The Pazzi Conspiracy:
The Plot against the Medici

HAROLD ACTON

The Pazzi Conspiracy: The Plot against the Medici

With 39 illustrations

THAMES AND HUDSON

To my friend Eva Neurath
fairy godmother of the visual arts
with love and gratitude

Text printed in Great Britain by
The Camelot Press, Southampton, Hampshire
Illustrations printed in Great Britain by
BAS Printers Limited, Wallop, Hampshire

Contents

Foreword

FOR better for worse – and I think for better – the Medici dominated Florence for three centuries, excepting two comparatively brief intervals. Though it seems to be modish to denigrate this remarkable family at present, their literary and aesthetic values have survived, and their monuments surround us materially as well as spiritually.

Lorenzo, known to history as the Magnificent, was the most versatile and talented member of his family, whose European status had been established by his grandfather Cosimo. Until his death in 1492 at the age of forty-three the executive in the Palazzo Vecchio, or Palace of the Priors, remained virtually under his control. As his most lucid biographer E. Armstrong pointed out, 'the period of Lorenzo's power may be divided into two almost equal halves. The first of these closes with the Pazzi Conspiracy.'

During its five-hundredth anniversary I thought it opportune to recall an event which had wider repercussions than the recent assassination of Signor Moro, one-time Premier of Italy. Fortunately it was a failure. Its result was the opposite of what the conspirators intended. Lorenzo rose like a phoenix from its ashes. Had it succeeded, the Medici would have been extinguished. Florence might then have fallen into the clutches of Girolamo Riario, the predatory nephew of Pope Sixtus IV, with the Pazzi as his satellites.

Until Professor Nicolai Rubinstein's long-awaited edition of Lorenzo's letters is published, I feel somewhat handicapped; but he tells me that they cast no new light on the Conspiracy. Therefore, at the risk of disappointing academics, I will not wander from the printed sources, though few witnesses agree about the details of Giuliano's murder. This is a story which interprets itself, and I leave the reader to draw his own conclusions.

My sources have been the oldest: Poliziano's *Conjurationis Pactianae Commentarium*, translated by Anicio Bonucci (1856) and Montesecco's Confession; Fabroni; Valori; Machiavelli's *Storie fiorentine*; Guicciardini's *Storia fiorentina*; Luca Landucci's *Diary*; Baron von Reumont's massive biography of Lorenzo; and Pieraccini's *La stirpe de'Medici di Cafaggiolo*. I have made liberal use of Janet Ross's *Lives of the Early Medici as told in their correspondence* (London 1910) with a few emendations. Among English biographies of Lorenzo the Magnificent E. Armstrong's (1896) still seems to me the best. Two volumes of Marsilio Ficino's letters have recently been translated by members of the Language Department of the School of Economic Science (Shepheard-Walwyn).

I

PRINCES OF THE FLORENTINE REPUBLIC

*Accession of Lorenzo and Giuliano de' Medici
to power*

FIFTEENTH-CENTURY Florence, like Venice, was only a nominal republic. It was governed by an oligarchy, a conservative burgher élite of rich bankers and merchants who were careful to preserve the semblance of a republic. The Albizzi family, for instance, had been in power since 1382 and had practically become a dictatorship under Rinaldo. His party might be labelled aristocratic in contrast with the popular party of the Medici, who had amassed an enormous fortune through banking and trade and spent liberally in support of the poorer classes – hence the loose talk of their 'corruption'.

Cosimo (1389–1464) had inherited his father Giovanni's business acumen with an extra dose of political ambition. Wealthier than his rival Rinaldo, he sought control of the chief magistracy, the Signoria, and the sporadic feud between them exploded in 1433 after the failure of hostilities against the town of Lucca. The Florentines, heavily taxed to pay for that wretched campaign, were thoroughly discontented, and the Albizzi suspected the Medici of fomenting sedition. Cosimo was arrested, imprisoned, and exiled to Padua, where he was treated 'not as a fugitive but as a prince'. During his detention in the tower of the Palazzo Vecchio he had narrowly escaped execution.

A year later the tables were turned on Rinaldo. Cosimo's recall was decreed by a new Signoria and he was welcomed like a conqueror on his arrival. Rinaldo degli Albizzi, his son, and about eighty of his collaborators were banished.

For the next thirty years Florence enjoyed the blessings of peace and prosperity under Cosimo, who preferred the reality of power to its externals. While the Palazzo Vecchio remained the seat of government, the invisible throne stood in the Palazzo Medici (now the Palazzo Riccardi). Cosimo ruled through committees whose election he controlled. Owing to the ramifications of his bank, his influence in Europe might be compared with that of the Rothschilds in a later era.

A tough, bred-in-the-bone Florentine who shrewdly shunned ostentation, he was admired and respected by the majority of his fellow citizens. In his foreign policy he broke with tradition by supporting Francesco Sforza's claims to the duchy of Milan, an alliance which was an important factor in the balance of power. Those who preferred Venice forgot that a Venetian monopoly would exclude Florentine wares from France, Germany, and the Adriatic.

Cosimo's private life was that of a munificent merchant-burgher and a discerning patron of art and scholarship. Benozzo Gozzoli's frescoes of the Procession of the Three Magi in Cosimo's palace chapel commemorate the Council of Eastern and Western Churches which he persuaded Pope Eugenius IV to hold in Florence (1439). Though the Council failed to unite the Churches it brought a galaxy of Greek scholars to Florence. One of these, Gemistos Plethon, influenced Cosimo to found the seminal Platonic Academy. Young Marsilio Ficino (1433–99), the son of a physician, became the leader of this new cult of spiritual love and beauty. After the Turkish conquest of Constantinople in 1453 so many Greek refugees were drawn to Florence that Poliziano remarked: 'Athens has not been destroyed by the barbarians but has migrated to Florence.'

Ficino produced the first complete translation of Plato from Greek into Latin (1463–70), considered universally to be a major event in the intellectual history of Europe, and his correspondence with other scholars extended to the rest of Italy and beyond it. The Platonic Academy held informal meetings in Cosimo's villa at Careggi, where

Ficino read his translation aloud as it progressed, to Cosimo's delight and edification.

'Greedy of time as Midas was of gold,' as Ficino said, Cosimo devoted increasingly more of it to the patronage of learning. 'I owe to Plato much,' Ficino added, 'to Cosimo no less. He realized for me the virtues of which Plato gave me the conception.' Though he suffered from arthritic gout – an illness inherited by his descendants – Cosimo's mind was lucid up to his death at Careggi on 1 August 1464, at the age of seventy-five. He wished to be buried without pomp in San Lorenzo. His tomb was simply inscribed *Pater Patriae*, by which he is always remembered.

Cosimo's favourite son, Giovanni, had predeceased him. His eldest son, Piero, was so crippled with gout that he was known as *Il Gottoso*, yet he had ample experience of politics at home and abroad. An ardent bibliophile and patron of the arts like his father, he was happily married to Lucrezia Tornabuoni, a Florentine of intellectual attainments, who bore him several daughters and two sons, Lorenzo and Giuliano, aged respectively fifteen and eleven when Cosimo died.

Unfortunately Cosimo had advised him to rely on the sagacity of his henchman Diotisalvi Neroni who proceeded to plot against him with Luca Pitti, Agnolo Acciaiuoli and Niccolò Soderini, all prominent citizens. Reporting that his finances were in a critical condition, Neroni recommended that outstanding loans should be called in. This sudden demand for payment caused several bankruptcies which naturally made Piero unpopular.

The conspirators had never approved of Cosimo's alliance with Milan, and when Francesco Sforza died in March 1466 they wanted to change this in favour of Venice. Luca Pitti's faction was called that of the Hill from the site of his palace; Piero's was that of the Plain. Pitti planned an armed insurrection with help from the Marquis of Ferrara and Piero was warned of this by his friend Giovanni Bentivoglio of Bologna. Although he was bedridden at Careggi, Piero appealed to the Milanese commander in the Romagna for support and was carried in a litter to Florence, which he reached safely in spite of an attempt to murder him. Lorenzo had gone ahead and, spotting the assassins, had sent him a message to take a different road.

Piero's unexpected return confounded the conspirators. Though the Signoria were pro-Hill they could not openly countenance an invasion from Ferrara. 'The Plain' was swarming with armed peasants from the Mugello and 'the Hill' hesitated to attack them until the Ferrarese forces arrived. In the meantime Luca Pitti had been furtively negotiating with Piero, who had promised to marry Lorenzo to one of his daughters – a promise never kept.

A pro-Medici Signoria entered office on 1 September and the four leading conspirators were condemned to death. The sentence was commuted to exile by Piero and Luca Pitti was pardoned. The exiles soon induced the Venetians to attack Florence but Bartolommeo Colleoni, the Venetian commander whose equestrian monument by Verrocchio is more famous than its subject, was trounced near Imola and peace was signed on 27 April 1468. At this period Piero bought the strategic town of Sarzana and the fortress of Sarzanello. He was far-sighted for all his physical disabilities.

During his adolescence Lorenzo was often sent on diplomatic missions – to Pisa to meet Federigo, the cultured younger son of King Ferrante of Naples; to Milan to represent his father at the marriage of Ferrante's eldest son to Francesco Sforza's clever daughter Ippolita, later to prove a loyal friend in need; to Bologna, Venice, Ferrara, Naples, and to Rome to congratulate Pope Paul II on his accession in 1466. On one of these missions Piero wrote to Lorenzo (11 May 1465): 'It is necessary for you now to be a man and not a boy; be so in words, deeds, and manners, and if you give dinners or other entertainments do not spare expense or whatever else is requisite for your honour.'

In words, deeds, and manners Lorenzo was a precocious adult, but he was boyish and typically Tuscan in his love of festivity. The

Carnival season had never been so exuberant; the tournaments on Piazza Santa Croce and the pageantry in honour of St John the Baptist, patron saint of Florence, were of a splendour never seen there before. All the talents contributed to the variety of these diversions which, as Vasari wrote, 'sharpened the wits of the contrivers while delighting the public'. On a material scale they reflected the ideas of the Platonic Academicians who were trying to reconcile Paganism with Christianity.

There was a particular poignancy in this hectic celebration of youth and springtime, as if the Medici brothers had premonitions that they would not make old bones. The Carnival songs attributed to Lorenzo could be matched in other languages, for their meaning was universal, whether an invocation to lasses and lads to 'get leave of your dads, and away to the Maypole hie', or

> Come, be gay
> While we may
> Beauty's a flow'r despised in decay;
> Youth's the season made for joys,
> Love is then a duty.

One of the most gorgeous tournaments was held before Lorenzo's marriage, nominally in honour of Lucrezia Donati, a famous beauty mistakenly supposed to be his mistress. Though Lorenzo was a skilled horseman it was the glamour of costumes, the orient pearl set in rubies and diamonds on his plumed cap (which was exchanged for a helmet with three blue feathers for the actual contest), and the velvet surcoat with the lilies of France on azure fringed with gold, which fascinated the spectators.

This was the heyday of allegory, of symbols and emblems whose meanings were infinitely flexible. Lorenzo entered the lists preceded by a knight who flourished his standard of white and purple taffeta. Andrea Verrocchio had painted it: a sun above, a rainbow below, with the legend *Le tems revient* (*sic*), signifying 'Time returns and the centuries are renewed.' Lucrezia Donati was depicted in the centre, her dress embroidered with gold and silver flowers. She was weaving a garland from a withered bay-tree which sprouted fresh leaves.

Other standards were also adorned with nymphs, one in white with a garland of rose-leaves, another gathering wind-blown beech leaves to feed a doe, another quenching the flaming darts of love in a fountain, and another breaking love's arrows and scattering their fragments in a field.

Even the horses wore trappings of velvet. It was a scene that appealed to the visual sophistication of the Florentines, who did not grudge Lorenzo the first prize. His record of the event is laconic: 'To follow the custom and do like others, I gave a tournament on Piazza S. Croce at great cost and with much magnificence: I find that about 10,000 gold florins were spent on it [in fact it cost much more]. Although I was no champion in the use of weapons and the delivery of blows the first prize was awarded to me, a helmet inlaid with silver and a figure of Mars as the crest.'

From Luigi Pulci's verses on that occasion we learn that there were eighteen competitors for the prize. The horse on which Lorenzo made his entry was presented to him by the King of Naples, the second which he mounted for the combat by the Marquis of Ferrara, while his armour was a gift from the Duke of Milan. At one stage his lance was broken, at another he cracked the helmet of his assailant, 'like a falcon plunging on his prey'.

Evidently he regarded it as a duty rather than a pleasure 'to follow the custom and do like others', for Lorenzo was not like others. His eyes and his voice commanded authority without arrogance or effort.

It was also his duty to marry for reasons of state, and his record of so important an event was equally laconic. 'I have taken a wife, or rather she was given to me . . .'

Lucrezia Tornabuoni, his mother, had gone to Rome to examine the young woman's qualifications, accompanied by her brother

Giovanni, head of the Medici bank there. The Orsini family, rivals of the Colonna, were almost as powerful as they were ancient and Clarice was eligible for many reasons, though she lacked the culture of Florentine girls of her age and equivalent rank. She was not a beauty, but Lucrezia's report of her was promising from a parental point of view. 'She is above medium stature and of fair complexion, and her manners are gentle if less gracious than ours. Being very modest, she would soon adapt herself to our customs. Her hair is not blonde for that is unusual here; her copious tresses have an auburn tint. Her face is somewhat round yet it does not displease me. Her neck is well shaped but seems to me rather thin. Her bosom was invisible for it is the fashion here to cover it, but it appears to be ample. Her hands are long and slender, and altogether we consider her above the average ...'

This was written to Lucrezia's husband, Piero 'the Gouty'. Lorenzo's uncle Francesco Tornabuoni, a partner in the Medici bank, sent him a more flowery description, urging him to write to 'the most perfect bride in Italy', while she was worried about his tournament. As soon as she heard that Lorenzo was unharmed and had distinguished himself with honour, she recovered her normal vivacity.

Lorenzo did not trouble to go and fetch her; his father's chronic ill health made his presence necessary at home. Clarice was escorted to Florence by Giuliano with a company of smart young cavaliers, and the marriage was celebrated in the Medici palace on 4 June 1469. For three days running there was a succession of banquets, and it was observed that the clothes were far grander than the dishes. Piero the Gouty never forgot his father's advice to avoid provoking the envy of fellow citizens. For the Medici (regarded as princes elsewhere) were still uncrowned citizens of the Republic and in Florence, as Francesco Guicciardini wrote, 'the citizens love equality, and yield unwillingly when they should acknowledge anyone as their superior.'

'As an example of moderation to others on such occasions,' wrote a guest, 'there was never more than one roast. In the morning a small dish, then some boiled meat, then a roast, after that wafers, marzipan and sugared almonds and pine seeds, then jars of preserved sweetmeats. In the evening jelly, a roast, fritters, wafers, almonds, and jars of sweetmeats . . . Of silver plate there was little . . .'

A stage hung with arras embroidered with Medici and Orsini arms had been erected outside the palace for dancing, and the bridegroom led the dance and chose the music, seconded by his handsome brother. Lorenzo could not be described as handsome. 'With regard to his personal appearance Nature had behaved to him like a stepmother,' it was said.

He was short-sighted with a broad nose and projecting jaw, but he had an athletic figure and, as his poems prove, his myopic eyes noticed everything worthy of note. In an age of pungent odours when few people washed, his lack of a sense of smell was a negative advantage. Though he was a dutiful husband he did not let marriage interfere with his pastimes. And he was a warm-blooded epicurean, keenly responsive to 'the principle of beauty in all things'. Affection grew with habit, but he never fell in love with his wife.

A few weeks after his wedding he deputized for his father at the Court of Milan, where a son had been born to the Duke on 20 June. Piero, too infirm to travel, reluctantly sent Lorenzo as his proxy. On previous missions he had told him to spare no expense, but now he advised him to avoid ostentation, though he was to present the Duchess with a gold necklace and a large diamond worth nearly 2000 ducats. 'Consequently the Duke wished me to stand godfather to all his future sons,' Lorenzo remarked.

The Duke Galeazzo Maria Sforza was as dissolute a specimen of despot as could then be found in Italy, conceited, rapacious and cruel. He loved the sound of his own voice and the shape of his hands, one of which may be seen pointing a long gloved index finger in his realistic portrait by Piero Pollaiuolo (now in the Uffizi). He could be ingratiating when it suited him, for Lorenzo wrote that he was 'entertained with more honour than the others who came for the same purpose, although they were better entitled to it than I.'

For so recent a bridegroom Lorenzo's letters to Clarice were perfunctory. Gentile Becchi, his former tutor who became Bishop of Arezzo, reported that he was in high spirits on the journey, welcomed with speeches and refreshments wherever they stopped. The Milanese court was riddled with domestic intrigue, but in spite of his moral depravity the Duke's policy was sound. He considered an alliance with the Medici essential to the peace of Italy.

After the theatrical pomp of the Sforza, Lorenzo was happy to return to the studious calm of Careggi. But his father was gradually succumbing to the rheumatic gout which had tormented him for years, and his illness was aggravated by worry over the state of Florence, where his partisans were shamelessly feathering their nests at his expense. From his bed of sickness he reprimanded them and threatened to recall the exiles. He had administered the foreign affairs of Tuscany until he died on 2 December 1469, at the age of fifty-three.

His brilliant sons had gained such popularity as his representatives that the ruling party invited them to succeed him as leaders of the State. Lorenzo was now aged twenty, his brother sixteen. In his diary Lorenzo confessed his reluctance to accept so arduous and dangerous a responsibility, but he realized that there was no alternative for a youth in his unusual position. His family and friends were counting on him and they must swim or sink together. 'In Florence it fares ill with the wealthy who do not govern,' he wrote. He and Giuliano were eloquently supported by Tommaso Soderini, who had helped to suppress the Neroni conspiracy against Piero in which his own brother Niccolò had been involved.

Some supposed that Soderini hoped to manipulate the Medici brothers as puppets. If so, he was badly mistaken. Lorenzo soon imposed his authority. He dealt patiently with applications for office and complaints of unfair taxation, and when a clique of malcontents attempted to capture the town of Prato they were quickly crushed and executed. The mayor of Prato, Cesare Petrucci, was to distinguish himself later during the Pazzi Conspiracy.

The Duke of Milan returned Lorenzo's visit in March 1471. Ostensibly he was to fulfil a vow to the shrine of the SS. Annunziata in thanksgiving for the birth of a son and heir. But his secret aim was to revive a Milanese protectorate over Florence's neighbours and to avert suspicions of his double-dealing which later events were to justify. He was already negotiating for the detachment of the Manfredi and Ordelaffi, lords of Faenza, Forlì and Imola, from their allegiance to Florence with a view to his daughter Caterina's future establishment. His ultimate ambition was to be crowned King of Lombardy.

He arrived with a formidable retinue. It was like an imperial progress: the ladies in litters of gold brocade, the courtiers bedizened with jewelled chains, some fifty grooms in liveries of silver cloth and damask tabards, a horde of attendants in silk or velvet hose, besides fifty chargers richly caparisoned, each led by a groom with the Sforza-Visconti arms on his doublet, and five hundred couples of greyhounds with huntsmen, falcons and falconers, a guard of a hundred knights and five hundred infantry. A train of 65–70 pack-mules carried the ducal strong-boxes, and a caravan of waggons with embroidered silk hoods brought up the rear. Man and beast, the entire procession covered nearly three miles.

The Duchess's suite included Galeazzo's mistress, the mother of his daughter Caterina whom she accompanied as *Madonna Nutrice* (Lady Foster-mother), and her complaisant husband Pietro Landriani, who acted as the Duchess's majordomo.

It was a flattering but extravagant invasion. The Duke and Duchess were Lorenzo's private guests, while their retinue were lodged at the expense of the Signoria. Considering that the season was Lent many were scandalized by the Duke's flouting of tradition, for he and his courtiers stuffed themselves with butcher's meat to the strains of fiddles and trumpets, and when the Church of Santo Spirito caught fire during a mystery play, 'The Descent of the Holy Ghost', this was generally attributed to Divine judgment – though the Duke was not present in person. The effect of this visit was said to be corrupting, for many young Florentines were tempted to emulate the sartorial eccentricities and moral laxity of the Milanese.

While Galeazzo had intended to dazzle his hosts, he was forced to admit that nothing in Milan could excel the Medici collection of works of art. According to the sixteenth-century historian, Scipione Ammirato, Galeazzo 'marvelled greatly at the numerous paintings by superlative masters, he being most partial to the painter's craft, whereof he swears he has seen more examples in the one palace of the Medici than in all the rest of Italy. Likewise, he added, 'tis certain their drawings and sculpture, and the marbles wrought by the ancients, are as wondrous as the craft of today, the jewellery, the books, and the other objects of exceeding rarity and value, looking upon which he deemed that any quantity of gold and silver should seem as mere dross in comparison.'

Precious vases of amethyst, agate, sardonyx, of crystal and jasper and lapis lazuli, gleamed in the twilight of Lorenzo's study. Though the reverse of pious, Galeazzo was deeply impressed by the private chapel which Benozzo Gozzoli had frescoed with a procession more sumptuous and exotic than his own. While he could appreciate painting he considered artists as menials, yet here they gathered sociably round Lorenzo to discuss their work with him in theory and practice, a familiarity which disconcerted him. Recently he had ordered an artist to paint the entire walls of a room within twenty-four hours. The creature had almost dropped dead with fatigue. That was Galeazzo's way with them! Whereas Lorenzo went so far as to invite them to his table.

The Duke frankly preferred the society of courtesans. Few women were safe from his impetuous assaults, and the docile Duchess had to wink at his philandering. In Florence he was obliged to curb such inclinations, for he was anxious to leave a favourable impression. Severe penalties were threatened against any of his suite who misbehaved. His liberality was flamboyant: the offer of a flower or two was rewarded with as many ducats, and he contributed no less than 2000 ducats to the restoration of the church which had been devastated by fire.

Well satisfied with his reception, the Duke departed on 23 March, assuring Lorenzo of his undying friendship. His long caravan returned by way of Lucca. Giuliano had ridden ahead to meet them at Massa and escort them as far as Sarzana. At Porto Venere they embarked on Genoese galleys, and Giuliano rode on to Genoa for a final leave-taking. The Florentines heaved sighs of relief and went back to their normal business, of which the apothecary Luca Landucci has left a graphic account in his diary, noting the current events, minor incidents of city life, market prices, weather and crops, which happened to claim his attention.

Lorenzo and Giuliano were able to spend more leisure in the country which they both preferred. They hunted in the Mugello, fished in the rivers, discussed crops with their farmers and plants with their gardeners, and while riding over the hills Lorenzo composed poems inspired by falconry and rustic life: the rhymed stanzas came to him easily as his spirits expanded in the pine-scented air. He relished the Tuscan folk songs and sayings, and it amused him to graft rustic idioms upon the classical periods of his prose. He had begun to create a new literature, different from that of the courtly school which had been cultivated by Italian writers hitherto.

Angelo Poliziano, the sixteen-year-old prodigy from Monte-pulciano, was to become a cherished member of his household, as dear to Giuliano as to Lorenzo. He could write Greek as well as Latin verse and he fused the spirit of both in his Italian compositions. Clarice disliked him, but her antipathy could not affect his growing prestige in literary circles. His unabashed paganism distressed the prim Roman matron. With Lorenzo and Giuliano he read Plato's 'Symposium' aloud and discussed the 'Platonic Theology' of his master Marsilio Ficino. They wandered into mythological mazes of allegory, reducing everything to symbols. The life of Socrates, for instance, was interpreted as a symbol of the life of Jesus. Souls were divided into categories, intellectual and universal, or sensitive, mortal and rational; and the latter into 'third essences' which animated nature – further subdivided into twelve orders, according to the twelve constellations of the zodiac. Through a hair-splitting analysis of 'third essences' they experienced thrills of discovery, peering into the future from a freshly excavated past, viewing politics as transitory and philosophy as eternal. With this amazing pupil of Ficino, who called him 'the Homeric boy', Lorenzo could also discuss poetic diction and technique, though Poliziano was five years younger – almost the same age as Giuliano.

This was a halcyon period for Florence. Through an elaborate system of sifting candidates for office in the Signoria the predominance of the Medicean party was assured. Despatches from foreign States were usually addressed to Lorenzo, 'sole mediator and representative of the Republic', as the King of Naples described him. And Lorenzo's steadfast purpose was to maintain the political balance of Italy.

2

LORENZO'S DISPUTES WITH POPE SIXTUS IV

Plot of the Pazzi and Girolamo Riario to exterminate the Medici

FEW tears were shed when the Venetian Pope Paul II died on 26 July 1471. His mania for antique bronzes, cameos and jewels was frowned upon by the Curia. It was notorious that he took rubies and sapphires to bed with him, which seemed like a superstition more pagan than spiritual. His contempt for literary sycophants had turned the pedants against him. He had dissolved the Roman Academy, but its members had ridiculed him and the Church, assuming clerical titles and parodying Christian rites. Pomponius Laetus, a scholar from Calabria, had even styled himself Pontifex Maximus, which did not amuse a person so conscious of his dignity. Platina, the Vatican librarian under Paul's successor, avenged them by writing his biography.

The election of a Pope of obscure origin and unblemished reputation was as agreeable to Lorenzo as to the Duke of Milan. Francesco of Savona, as he was called before adopting the proud surname of Rovere (signifying oak), had been General of the Franciscan Order, then Cardinal of S. Pietro in Vincoli for four years, yet too poor to restore his palace near that venerable basilica where the chains that bound St Peter are preserved. He was crowned under the title of Sixtus IV on 25 August, at the age of fifty-seven, receiving the tiara of Gregory the Great from the hands of Cardinal Borgia. A shadow was cast on the ceremony by the turbulence of the Roman mob. Infuriated because his cavalcade had caused a crush, they threw stones at the new Pope's litter – an incident that did not seem auspicious.

When Lorenzo accompanied the Florentine embassy to congra-tulate Sixtus, he was given so cordial a reception that the Duke of Milan took umbrage. The first fruits of this cordiality were profitable, for the funds of the Roman Depository or Receiver's Office were transferred to the Medici bank under Lorenzo's uncle Giovanni Tornabuoni, together with privileges in mining the alum of Tolfa near Civitavecchia. No doubt Cardinal Orsini, who had supported the Pope's election, was partly responsible for this preferential treatment. Lorenzo was delighted with the gifts of two antique marble busts of Augustus and Agrippa, as well as an engraved chalcedony vase and various cameos and medals from Paul II's collection which he had been allowed to buy at a discount. He had hoped also to obtain a Cardinal's hat for his brother, but the Pope was politely evasive on the subject.

It soon became apparent that the Franciscan theologian was an antithesis of the patron saint of poverty. He adapted himself strenuously to the prevailing current. To increase the temporal power of the Papacy became his obsession. His nepotism was quite logical: he could trust his next-of-kin better than his curial entourage. A flock of poor relations from Savona rallied round the spreading oak with golden acorns.

Sixtus lost no time in promoting two of his nephews to the Cardinalate: Giuliano della Rovere, aged twenty-eight, and his sister's son Pietro Riario, aged twenty-five. Pietro, his favourite, became a Croesus overnight, and until he died three years later his extravagance was a byword throughout Italy. Another nephew, Leonardo, was appointed Prefect of Rome and married an illegitimate daughter of King Ferrante of Naples. Within a few years these were able to accumulate undreamt-of wealth while senior Cardinals looked on with impotent disgust.

Early the following year a revolt in Volterra endangered the peace for which Lorenzo was striving. The Volterrans had a long history of turmoil until, exhausted by internal feuds, they sought security in the protectorate of Florence. Their intermittent cravings for independence exploded again in 1472 owing to a concession to mine alum in their territory. Though the mine was unprofitable they protested against the lease of public property to a private company, expelled its workmen and closed it. The Florentines regarded this as an infringement of their sovereignty, while the company, of which two Volterrans were directors, clamoured for their rights. One of these, Paolo Inghirami, was thrown from a window on his return from Florence, and the municipality threatened to appeal for foreign intervention.

Against the cautious advice of Tommaso Soderini, Lorenzo decided to set an example to other potential rebels. The most estimable of condottieri, Federigo da Montefeltro of Urbino, was engaged to attack Volterra with a force of some 5,500 mercenaries, and smaller contingents were sent by the Duke of Milan and the Pope. Volterra's ill-paid troops refused to fight and there was chaos inside the town. After twenty-five days' siege a treacherous guard admitted the Milanese through a breach in the walls. Federigo's troops followed, and even he could not restrain their lust for pillage. Though he hanged the ringleaders the city was sacked with barbarous brutality. An earthquake or landslide increased the desolation.

Lorenzo visited the ravaged town and administered what relief he could. The massive fortress which still dominates the landscape was built over the ruins of the Bishop's palace and the Church of S. Pietro, a grim memorial. Lorenzo was never forgiven by the Volterrans and historians have blamed him, instead of Federigo's mercenaries, for the sack. But according to contemporary standards his credit was enhanced. He was not, as has been alleged, a shareholder in the alum company. Personally he remained convinced that the conflict might have proliferated beyond Tuscany.

Pope Sixtus, who had seemed so amiably disposed towards Lorenzo, was too busy advancing the fortunes of his own family to bother about Lorenzo's application on behalf of Giuliano. Lorenzo wrote to remind the Pope of the 'long-standing desire of our house to have a Cardinal', and Jacopo Ammannati, Cardinal of Pavia, offered friendly advice and support. Supposing any accident should happen to Lorenzo, he wrote, 'and Giuliano were in the position we are striving for while your children were still young, it seems to me your house would be in danger of losing the pre-eminence left by Cosimo to Piero, and from Piero to you, and with the pre-eminence lose the wealth, and thus close the door against your successors. On the other hand, there is the prestige which would be acquired by the enhanced dignity of Giuliano, the assistance he might render to your State, and the certainty of gaining a trustworthy addition to the College. . . . Speaking for myself, nothing would be more pleasing than to have the company of Giuliano, and possessing such a pledge, we should be entitled to expect loyal assistance from your State. His cheerful nature would increase our happiness.'

The Pope replied tactfully to the Signoria regretting the delay but assuring them that at the next creation of Cardinals, when the just demands of others were satisfied, 'we shall have regard to your Republic also, especially if it approves our choice'. As Giuliano was a layman under twenty he could afford to wait. (Later, when the Pope's seventeen-year-old great-nephew Raffaello Sansoni was elected, adolescence was no impediment.)

Giuliano's genial temper and fine physique endeared him above all to the ladies and, like Lorenzo, he was a precocious amorist; but so were the Papal nephews. Whether his devotion to the beautiful Simonetta Cattaneo was platonic or not, their names were linked romantically by rumour. He dedicated poems to her, but that was merely a literary convention. Giuliano shared Lorenzo's tastes without meddling in the government. Poliziano called him 'the delight of

Florentine youth' and as 'the prince of youth' he was complementary to Lorenzo. Equally robust in his zest for life, an athlete who had trained himself to endure hunger and thirst, he was a natural arbiter of the younger generation. Botticelli portrayed him in a pensive mood, delicately disdainful: heavy-lidded eyes with an inward gaze, a Grecian nose, with wavy dark hair swept back from a high forehead and an olive complexion. Surrounded by a posse of boisterous companions, whose practical jokes were often crude and sometimes cruel, he never realized how many of those who fawned on him were jealous of his popularity.

Among the old Florentine patricians the Pazzi family had watched the growing power of the Medici with smouldering resentment, and the Pazzi were still their keenest competitors in finance. Intermarriage had seemed the most practical way to conciliate them. Lorenzo's favourite sister Bianca was married to Guglielmo de' Pazzi and bore her husband fifteen children. In spite of this connection, the Pazzi remained surreptitious rivals.

Owing to their nobility, the Pazzi had lost their civic rights by the punitive legislation of the so-called *Ordinamenti della Giustizia* in 1293. But these had been restored by Lorenzo's grandfather, and two Pazzi brothers had held the office of Gonfalonier, chief of the Signoria. Even so, they were too overbearing to be popular and they blamed Lorenzo because they had been kept out of office since his father's death. A retrospective law giving preference to collateral males over daughters in case of intestacy was also attributed to Lorenzo and increased the Pazzi's rancour. Guglielmo's second brother Giovanni, who had married the only daughter of wealthy Borromeo, felt unjustly defrauded in consequence; Borromeo having left no will, his estate passed to his nephews instead of to his daughter.

Giuliano is said to have warned Lorenzo that this might lead to friction. Guglielmo's third brother, Francesco, was so enraged that he settled in Rome, where he governed the Pazzi bank very profitably.

Lorenzo seemed unaware of his animosity. For the time being his enthusiasm was concentrated on the improvement of education. The Signoria having decided that Pisa was better adapted to a university than Florence, Lorenzo went there to organize new courses under the best available teachers for higher salaries than were paid elsewhere. Accompanied by Poliziano, he was able to combine intellectual pastimes with hawking and hunting roe deer, while his pregnant wife moped at home. Poliziano described his diversions in tantalizing letters to Clarice, reporting Lorenzo's delight in a peregrine falcon 'which came back to the lure most obediently' and the recovery of another precious falcon which had been lost. The Ferrarese ambassador wrote to his master in the same strain: 'unless things change there will be more news of battles between birds and dogs than of armies and doughty deeds.' As usual, distinguished visitors were entertained with appropriate ceremony. King Christian of Denmark was most edified by the Greek manuscripts of the Gospels, 'the true treasures of princes', as he observed.

Giuliano's tournament in 1475 was another gala occasion, even more spectacular than Lorenzo's in 1469. Just as Lorenzo's had been held under the patronage of Lucrezia Donati, Giuliano's was dedicated to the lovely Simonetta, wife of Marco Vespucci. This was no more than a compliment to feminine beauty: in spite of gossip it did not signify they were lovers. The lady was to die of consumption a year later.

Poliziano's *Stanze* to commemorate the joust were to influence such painters as Botticelli as well as the lyric poets, although they were never completed – perhaps on account of Simonetta's premature death. A description of the birth of Venus in the first book is almost identical with Botticelli's painting. But if the actual joust is not described in the poem, there are other records of the 'tilting furniture' of the combatants who entered the lists. Giuliano's equipage included a knight on horseback who bore a standard of Alexandrine taffeta: in the upper part of it was a sun, in the centre a tall figure of Pallas in a golden tunic reaching down to the knees, and under the tunic was a white vestment powdered with gold. The feet stood on two flames of fire whence other flames issued to consume olive branches. Over her head was a burnished morion of antique form, and her braided tresses fluttered in the breeze. Her right hand held a tilting-lance and her left hand the shield of Medusa. Around her was a field of variegated flowers, containing the stump of an olive tree to which the god of love was bound by a golden cord. His bow, quiver, and broken arrows lay at his feet. Andrea Verrocchio had painted it, and his superb helmet surmounted by a winged dragon, now in the Bargello, was probably a relic of the same joust. Botticelli designed similar standards and accoutrements, and their allegorical themes were usually suggested, if not invented, by Poliziano, the Medicean laureate. Verrocchio's terracotta bust of Giuliano in ornate armour must have been modelled at the same period: a mask of Medusa scowls open-mouthed from the breastplate and the young man's expression is that of a victorious athlete. A cardinal's hat would have been incongruous on such a head.

Giuliano was eminently endowed for worldly pleasures, but so were the Pope's nephews, whose prodigality contrasted with their former penury. Pietro Riario had held tournaments on a grander scale in Rome, and the luxury of his banquets rivalled those of Nero. Classical allegories were introduced into his kitchen. Roast peacocks were served with their fan-tails open beside a figure of Orpheus with his lyre. Other courses, which required four lusty pages to carry them, represented Perseus, Andromeda and the dragon, or the race of Atalanta. Before each dish a seneschal appeared in different uniform on horseback and a different sennet was sounded. A joust usually followed the banquet.

But Cardinal Riario had died of his excesses in 1474, after assuming the archbishopric of Florence and visiting his other sees as Umbrian legate. He had left the government of each new diocese to a deputy while enjoying its pecuniary and social advantages. The Duke of Milan, still aspiring to the crown of Lombardy, had promised to support him at the next conclave, and even the Pope's resignation in favour of this nephew had been mooted. The Duke then agreed to sell Imola to the Pope instead of to Lorenzo, as he had promised.

Though the Pope's intensity of grief at the death seemed exaggerated to the Curia, the Cardinal's brother Girolamo soon replaced him in his favour, if not in his deepest affections. Being a layman equally grasping and ambitious, Girolamo was a greater menace to Lorenzo. The strategic city of Imola was to be the first stage in a progressive annexation of the Romagna; Forlì and Faenza were next in line.

When he discovered from Francesco de' Pazzi that Lorenzo had tried to prevent him from raising the purchase money for Imola, the Pope transferred the Curia's account from the Medici bank to that of the Pazzi, who had advanced three-fourths of the sum required. Girolamo aggravated his uncle's annoyance with Lorenzo. While Cardinal Giuliano della Rovere, the most martial of the Pope's nephews, was waging war on the petty tyrants of Umbria, the Florentines had to protect their frontiers from hostile incursions. Lorenzo was accused of backing Niccolò Vitelli, when he resisted the Papal troops at Città di Castello. Though Lorenzo denied this the Pope was too prejudiced to believe him.

Deeply as Lorenzo resented the underhand sale of Imola, which would have been an asset to Florence, he never quarrelled with the slippery Duke of Milan, and his correspondence with the Pope was diplomatically deferential. To keep the peace he formed a league with Milan and Venice, but the Pope and his new ally, the King of Naples, refused to join it, suspecting a coalition against the Holy See.

Instead of opposing Cardinal Riario's appointment to the archbishopric of Florence, Lorenzo had given him a sumptuous reception, but the choice of Francesco Salviati as his successor was obnoxious for various reasons apart from his known antagonism to the Medici. The Pope compromised by appointing Rinaldo Orsini, Lorenzo's brother-in-law, to the vacant see. The frustrated Salviati continued to intrigue with the papal nephews, and in spite of Florentine protests he was awarded the archbishopric of Pisa as a consolation. In retaliation, the Florentine Signoria prevented him from occupying his new see for three years. It would have suited Salviati to make mischief among disaffected Pisans, especially in the university. According to Poliziano, he was steeped in every vice and a 'contemner of every law, human and divine.' While kicking his heels in Rome he was able to foment the Pope's hatred of the Medici. No more was said about Giuliano's seat in the Sacred College.

So far, Lorenzo had been fortunate in obtaining the military cooperation of Federigo of Urbino, but the Pope proceeded to alienate him from Florentine service by loading him with titles and honours. Besides appointing him Captain-General of the Papal army, he created him a duke and a knight of St Peter at an elaborate ceremony in August 1474. After the *Gloria* at High Mass, Girolamo Riario and Giovanni della Rovere escorted him to the Papal throne. While Federigo knelt on the steps Sixtus took the sword of St Peter from his nephews, blessed it and handed it to him with an injunction to wield it against the enemies of Christ. Cardinal Orsini fastened it on his belt; the nephews buckled on his golden spurs; then, at a signal from the master of ceremonies, he drew it from its scabbard and brandished it twice. Before the reading of the Gospel his knightly mantle of gold brocade was replaced by a ducal robe of the same material. After the Gospel he was led again before the Pope, who hung a gold chain round his neck, placed a ducal cap on his head, and offered him a sceptre with further benedictions. Federigo pronounced an oath of fidelity, prostrated himself before Sixtus and kissed his feet and hands while he recited special prayers, and then embraced him. After kissing all the Cardinals present and saluting the chairs of those absent, Federigo knelt again before Sixtus, who consigned to him two standards, one with the arms of the Church, the other with his own, declaring him Captain-General.

1 This view of Medicean Florence, with the familiar landmarks of the Duomo and the Baptistry, is a detail from a painting of the Crucifixion by Sandro Botticelli, who was active in Florence at the time of the Pazzi Conspiracy.

2 The actual governing of Florence was nominally in the hands of the elected Signoria, whose meetings and deliberations took place in the Palace of the Signoria (now more often called Palazzo Vecchio), seen here in an anonymous painting of the last decade of the fifteenth century.

3 Cosimo de' Medici (1389–1464) was the first of that family to achieve political power in Florence, which was then handed down from generation to generation.

4 Francesco Sforza, the condottiere who became Duke of Milan in 1450 following the death of the last Visconti. Cosimo's alliance with him was his original contribution to Florentine foreign policy.

5 Botticelli's *Adoration of the Magi* is traditionally held to contain portraits of
Cosimo de' Medici (kneeling before the Child), his son Piero the Gouty (in the
centre beneath the Virgin) looking at his brother Giovanni, next to whom stands
Giuliano, Piero's son and brother of Lorenzo the Magnificent (at the left, with
sword).

6 Lorenzo the Magnificent, the towering Renaissance figure who controlled the destiny of Florence from 1469 to 1492; a terracotta bust made by Andrea del Verrocchio around 1485.

7 Verrocchio also made a bust of
Lorenzo's brother, Giuliano, victim of
the Pazzi Conspiracy.

8 This iron helmet with an ornamental
dragon is supposed to have been made by
Verrocchio to be worn by Lorenzo
during a festive tournament.

9 Verrocchio's most famous masterpiece
is the monument to Bartolommeo
Colleoni, the Venetian condottiere who
was defeated in 1468 by Florentine forces
supporting the Medici faction.

10, 11 The subjects of these two Botticelli portraits are Giuliano de' Medici and possibly Simonetta Cattaneo, the wife of Marco Vespucci, who was rumoured to be Giuliano's mistress.

12 This detail of a *cassone* painting of the late fourteenth century shows the Florentine guilds and confraternities carrying their distinctive banners in a procession to the Baptistry during the festival of St John the Baptist.

13 A tournament in Medicean Florence, taking place in the Piazza Santa Croce; from a *cassone* painting.

14, 15 Two woodcuts from the love poem 'La Giostra', by Angelo Poliziano, the young poet who became a favourite in the Medici household during Lorenzo's lifetime. The upper illustration is of an armed cavalier riding a unicorn; the lower shows Giuliano worshipping Venus.

16, 17 The palaces in Florence of the Pazzi and Medici families. The Medici palace (below), designed by Michelozzo, was the earlier, having begun construction around 1440, in Cosimo's time. The architect of the Pazzi home (left) was probably Giuliano da Maiano, and it was built between 1462 and 1470.

18, 19 Brunelleschi was the architect of the Pazzi chapel, attached to the Church of Santa Croce, Florence: left, interior view; below, the entrance from the cloister.

Next day Giovanna, one of Federigo's daughters, was married to the Pope's nephew Giovanni, thus founding a della Rovere dynasty at Urbino. More honours were showered on Federigo by the King of Naples, and from England he received the Order of the Garter. By modern standards his military renown was exaggerated, for the warfare of that age was conducted like a languid game of chess until the plunder of a city was promised to the troops. The devastation of Volterra had had copious precedents under other condottieri, as when Francesco Sforza allowed his soldiers to sack Piacenza for four days running. Inevitably mercenaries were opportunists: their political morality should not be judged by ours. Federigo was exceptional for his culture. He devoted his professional profits to the improvement of Urbino, which he governed wisely and well. His court was regarded as a perfect academy of military education. Under his son Guidobaldo its fame was publicized by Castiglione's *Courtier*.

A discriminating collector of rare manuscripts – he despised printed books – Federigo had more tastes in common with the Medici than with Sixtus IV and his parvenu nephews.

Federigo's defection was a serious blow to Lorenzo but he would not allow politics to depress him unduly. He and Giuliano were deeply attached to their mother Lucrezia, who was always a great moral support. Her religious poems expressed the mystical side of her nature but she was also a practical housekeeper. Immensely charitable, she was approached by all sorts of applicants for her mediation and assistance. Poliziano revered her and kept her informed of events when she was taking a cure for arthritis at Bagno a Morba near Volterra. With Clarice he was never on the same close terms. As a Roman aristocrat full of family pride and bigotry, she despised him for his humble origin. A conscientious mother and a submissive wife, she could not sympathize with Lorenzo's intellectual bent. From her querulous letters it is plain that she felt neglected while Lorenzo and Giuliano went on hunting expeditions. Privately she was upset by

Lorenzo's cynical attitude to the Pope, for she could not distinguish between the Holy See and the unholiness of its present incumbent.

Lorenzo and Giuliano went their primrose ways unconscious of any latent animosity. They were even on polite terms with Girolamo Riario, now lord of the Imola they had coveted. They failed to realize how profoundly the Pope had been incensed against them. Whenever there was a disturbance in the Romagna he blamed them.

The sack of Volterra had confirmed Lorenzo's dislike of war, and in Florence the blessings of peace were abundantly clear. In a letter to Clarice, Poliziano described a typical holiday excursion with Lorenzo, 'singing all the way, and occasionally talking of holy things so as not to forget Lent ... Lorenzo is brilliant and he enlivens the whole company. Yesterday I counted twenty-six horses of those accompanying him. When we reached San Miniato [al Tedesco] last evening we began to read a few passages of St Augustine, then the reading resolved itself into music, and watching and guiding the evolutions of a famous dancer who is here.'

With her children at Cafaggiolo, Clarice's amusements were limited. Little wonder she grumbled when Poliziano tried to teach them the classics. She considered it far more important to learn the Roman breviary by heart. Those lecherous old pagans could only lead the young astray.

Lorenzo put too much faith in the league which Sixtus refused to join and relied on the Duke of Milan, who for all his deviousness had a stable government: his vices were those of other Italian despots on a grosser scale, combining patronage of the arts with narcissistic vanity and pious observances with barbarity. While he forbade trading on Sundays and saints' days, and took pains to perfect the choir of his private chapel, he thought nothing of committing adultery whenever he felt inclined. The news of his murder came as a shock not only to Lorenzo but also to the Pope, who exclaimed prophetically: 'The peace of Italy is dead.'

On 26 December 1476, Galeazzo Maria Sforza was stabbed to death as he entered the Church of Santo Stefano in Milan. The three assassins, Carlo Visconti, Girolamo Olgiati and Giannandrea Lampugnani, had rehearsed their act in advance and prayed fervently to Saints Ambrose and Stephen to bless it. They were instigated by Cola Montano, a teacher of rhetoric, who had preached the glory of tyrannicide with illustrations from Greek and Roman history. In spite of sinister omens and presentiments the Duke went to Mass as usual on the feast of St Stephen. The conspirators were awaiting him at the door. Lampugnani knelt before him as if to present a petition and plunged a dagger into his belly. The accomplices finished him off. Having tripped over a lady's gown, Lampugnani was killed on the spot; his fellow conspirators were captured a few days later and beheaded after hideous torture. They inspired no sympathy and no insurrection followed. Lampugnani's corpse was dragged through the streets amid howls of execration. Olgiati, an ardent republican, composed an apologia in Latin declaring that he would gladly suffer greater torments for so noble a cause. Far from rejoicing, the Milanese regretted their tyrant, who amongst other advantages had introduced the cultivation of rice into their land. Bona of Savoy, the Duke's widow, implored the Pope to grant him posthumous absolution, and his sins were atoned for by a bountiful subsidy to the Holy See.

Lorenzo sent envoys to condole with the Duchess and to assure her of his solidarity, but she could not hold her own against the intrigues of her quarrelsome brothers-in-law. Lorenzo had lost a substantial ally. Elsewhere the Duke's murder was commended by the most fanatical humanists. 'It was a worthy, laudable, and virile deed,' wrote Alamanno Rinuccini, 'which should be imitated by all who live under a tyrant or anything similar.' He blamed the cowardice and degradation of Sforza's subjects because 'the example bore little or no fruit and those who had acted nobly should suffer death. Nevertheless they had freed the earth from an infamous monster.'

The repercussions of this noble act, however, were disastrous for Italy. Ultimately it led to the French invasion. Murder in churches became fashionable. There was less risk in stabbing the victim in a holy place of worship; and since the assassins could claim classical precedents they found magniloquent apologists in men of culture. Then as now, the mask of freedom was often worn by hypocrites. In the case of the so-called Pazzi Conspiracy the reality under the mask has been dramatically revealed.

This conspiracy was concocted in Rome under the tolerant nose of Pope Sixtus IV. Girolamo Riario, always profuse in expressions of goodwill to the Magnificent Lorenzo, hated him as the chief obstacle to his ambitions in the Romagna and farther afield. He realized he must make hay while the sun shone and his uncle was still alive. Since his marriage to Caterina Sforza, the legitimized bastard of the murdered Duke, his ambitions had swollen considerably. An energetic amazon of sixteen, his bride was equally ambitious. Sixtus was altogether charmed by her, and she was to prove a congenial mate, more virile than her husband. Imola was too provincial for her, and until Girolamo possessed Forlì she stayed in Rome, which provided her with the amusements she cared for, such as hunting in the Campagna.

While Caterina coquetted with the Pope, Girolamo kept his anger with Lorenzo on the boil. Sixtus still held Lorenzo responsible for helping Niccolò Vitelli to defend Città di Castello – 'the scandalous support of a rebellious vassal' – though Lorenzo protested: 'Be assured, Holy Father, I reckon the favour of your Holiness among the greatest of my treasures, and I have no desire to lose it for the sake of Messer Niccolò or anyone else.' But Lorenzo's private thoughts were sent in a letter to Baccio Ugolini: 'As far as I am concerned I think it would be preferable for the power to be divided, and if it could be done without scandal, I would prefer three or four Popes to one Pope.'

The lingering presence of Francesco Salviati in Rome after he had been appointed archbishop of Pisa was an additional cause of vexation, and in 1477 Sixtus became convinced that Lorenzo had instigated the madcap condottiere Carlo Fortebraccio, then in the Venetian service, to attack Perugia and raid Sienese territory when in fact Lorenzo had urged him to withdraw his troops. Lorenzo's alliance with Venice also annoyed Naples on account of their commercial rivalry. Yet when King Ferrante remarried in the same year, Lorenzo spared no expense to entertain his daughter, the Duchess of Ferrara, at Pisa on her way to the wedding, and the Duchess was captivated by his brilliance. Henceforth he could rely on her friendship at the court of Naples, where the Pope had more partisans.

Girolamo Riario, alarmed for his own future, decided that there was only one solution to his problems: the Medici brothers would have to be exterminated. Knowing Francesco de' Pazzi's hostility to his brothers-in-law, he took him into his confidence. Franceschino, as he was nicknamed, was a pugnacious little bachelor of thirty-four, inordinately proud of his ancient lineage. He cherished an illusion that if the Medici were out of their way the Pazzi would be welcomed as liberators by the Florentines. He was therefore entirely in sympathy with Riario's proposal, delighted to find so powerful a confederate. Franceschino visualized a Pazzi usurpation; Riario a Papal one with himself at the helm. Each intended to exploit the other for his private designs. Franceschino proposed to deal with the murders, while Riario could order an expeditionary force from Imola to occupy Florence in the following confusion.

An eager accomplice was at hand in the archbishop-designate of Pisa still kicking his heels in Rome. The ancient Salviati family were also connected with the Pazzi. But the collaboration of Francesco's uncle Jacopo, head of the clan in Florence, was indispensable. Riario could vouch for that of his uncle the Pope.

Jacopo de' Pazzi had held the office of Gonfalonier in 1469: a cantankerous old gambler, haughty and avaricious, superficially he remained on good terms with Lorenzo though he despised his régime.

He was a shrewd realist, however, and when Franceschino confided his plan to him his gambling instinct deserted him. He retorted bluntly that the plot was doomed to failure. Though violent, Jacopo was opposed to any violence which might lead to the ruin of his family. The Medici had thrust deep roots in Florence; their partisans were legion . . .

Franceschino attributed his uncle's objections to the defeatism of a crusty old man. If he could show him that he was backed by military force Jacopo would be converted.

On returning to Rome Francesco conferred with Archbishop Salviati and together they proceeded to sound Giovanni Battista da Montesecco, an experienced condottiere in the service of the Pope and Count Riario. Having fought successfully for Pope Paul II against Roberto Malatesta of Rimini in 1469, Montesecco was used to bloodshed. But this was different. What these men now proposed to him seemed a private enterprise, distinct from his official duties. He was a captain of mercenaries, not a common cut-throat. Francesco and the Archbishop explained that they were negotiating on behalf of the Pope and Count Riario who were exasperated by Lorenzo's behaviour, quoting chapter and verse, from his support of Vitelli to that of Fortebraccio, Montesecco's professional rivals. As long as Lorenzo and his brother were alive Count Riario's status was 'not worth a bean'. Montesecco stood on his dignity: he would await Count Riario's instructions.

In due course Riario summoned Montesecco in Salviati's presence and demanded his opinion of the scheme previously discussed with Francesco de' Pazzi. 'I can offer no opinion till I hear how you intend to carry it out,' he replied. The Count and the Archbishop enumerated their grievances against Lorenzo but Montesecco was stubborn. How were those grievances to be redressed? After some hesitation they blurted it out: the murder of Lorenzo and Giuliano, combined with a military invasion. The Florentines groaned under the despotism of the Medici; they were ready for a revolution. On the other hand the Pazzi and Salviati enjoyed such prestige that the whole city would rise in their favour. Montesecco remained sceptical. Albeit no politician, he was aware of Lorenzo's fame at home and abroad. 'Take care, my lords,' he said, 'for Florence is a mighty undertaking.'

Both the Count and the Archbishop contradicted him. 'We know more than you about the state of Florence. Our success is as certain as our meeting here today. Meanwhile it is essential to convert Messer Jacopo de' Pazzi to the cause. When we melt that block of ice the deed is half done.'

What were the views of His Holiness? As the Pope's captain Montesecco would not move without his sanction.

The Count and the Archbishop reassured him that the Pope was even more anxious than they for this practical conclusion. Lorenzo had given him too many provocations: he would approve of whatever they decided for the best. The matter had already been discussed with him. If Montesecco had the slightest qualms, they would arrange a private audience, and he would have the privilege of hearing the Pope's decision from his own lips.

Montesecco's subsequent account of his conference with Sixtus IV is absolutely trustworthy, since he was on the verge of execution and had no reason to lie. Sixtus told him that a change of government in Florence would be most agreeable to him but that it was to involve no bloodshed. Montesecco argued that this could not be achieved without the death of Lorenzo and Giuliano, and perhaps of others as well. 'I do not want the death of anyone in any circumstances,' the Pope insisted, 'since that would be contrary to our holy office. Though Lorenzo is a despicable villain who has treated us shamefully we have no desire for his death, but only for a change of government.'

Count Riario interjected: 'We shall do everything possible to avoid bloodshed, but if it should happen, would Your Holiness pardon the offender?'

The Pope replied impatiently: 'You are a brute. I repeat I desire the death of no man but only a change of government. And I tell you, Gian Battista, that I urgently desire that the government of Florence be removed from Lorenzo, for he is a treacherous scoundrel who consistently defies us. As soon as he is removed we may deal as we please with the Republic, which will be highly agreeable to us.'

The Count and the Archbishop concurred. When Florence was at his disposal the Pope could dominate the whole of Italy, and everybody would compete for his alliance. 'Depend on us to do all that is needful to attain this end.'

The Pope repeated his former injunction with emphasis, adding that he would supply whatever troops were required. This sounded ambiguous after his proviso that there was to be no bloodshed. Before retiring the Archbishop said: 'Holy Father, are you content that we should steer this vessel? We shall steer it safely to port.'

'I am content. But take heed that the honour of the Holy See and of the Count is not compromised.'

Accordingly Montesecco attended to the military details. Several mercenary captains were available in the Romagna, and each was warned to muster contingents at strategic points, though nothing was said about the ultimate plan. Montesecco was then sent to Lorenzo in Florence on a mission of spurious goodwill: the tyrant was to be duped by conciliatory messages.

After his long ride to the remote villa of Cafaggiolo, Montesecco was disarmed by Lorenzo's affability. This debonair gentleman was totally unlike the reptile he had been led to expect. Lorenzo betrayed no antagonism to Count Riario, of whom he spoke with bland urbanity. Ever hospitable, Lorenzo invited Montesecco to an excellent repast, showed him his stables, discussed the points of his horses and the produce of his farms. He had none of the haughtiness of Montesecco's patrons in Rome. Altogether he was strangely sympathetic. Even his grooms and retainers were conscious of this as he bandied jokes with them. The peasants looked prosperous in their kilted tunics and leather gaiters, singing lustily as they drove their bullock carts. The women were spinning and plaiting straw hats in the sunshine. 'I love the country,' Lorenzo said, 'but I am forced to spend more time in the city. Another glass of wine for the road?' Already Montesecco flinched from the prospect of having to kill him.

Reluctantly he rode back to Florence where he had an appointment with Jacopo de' Pazzi. Even after scrutinizing his letters of credence from Count Riario and Archbishop Salviati, old Jacopo's response was negative. 'They will break their necks,' he said. 'I understand our affairs much better than they do in Rome. I wish to hear no more about this business.'

But when Montesecco reported his interview with the Pope, Jacopo began to thaw. If His Holiness had agreed to send troops he must surely approve of the conspiracy. 'Though it were deplorable, an affair of such consequence could only be settled by the murder of Lorenzo and Giuliano.'

While Montesecco was in charge of military operations, the Archbishop would have to co-ordinate the details of the double assassination. Several accomplices were required to deal with the brothers separately yet simultaneously, if possible out of doors. Giuliano might be travelling to Piombino as there was a prospect of his engagement to a daughter of the ruling Appiani: this might offer an opportunity. To kill the Medici brothers together in Florence seemed too hazardous. Francesco thought it could be done whenever and wherever they were caught off their guard, either at a banquet or in church.

Montesecco returned to Rome to report his satisfactory progress to Riario and the Archbishop. Although the latter was not *persona grata* in Florence, he invented a pretext to visit Lorenzo. Carlo Manfredi, the lord of Faenza, was dangerously ill and since Riario coveted his land, Salviati might discuss its future with Lorenzo, pretending to agree with his views. After inspecting the troops at Imola, Montesecco joined him at the Pazzi villa outside the city. No time should be lost, he said, if the troops were to co-ordinate their invasion with the double murder. But in spite of all their efforts their emissaries had failed to find an opportunity. Military manoeuvres were suspended until this occurred, and at the end of the year the plot was postponed.

3

MURDER OF GIULIANO DE' MEDICI IN THE CATHEDRAL
Punishment of the conspirators

EARLY in 1478 Girolamo Riario decided to decoy Lorenzo to Rome. 'I have not the slightest doubt', he wrote to him on 15 January, 'that the Holy Father will welcome you with open arms while I, owing to the affection inspired by our friendly relations, am entirely prepared to gratify your Magnificence and whatever grievances may have arisen will vanish.'

Confident in Lorenzo's acceptance, Riario told Montesecco that the cat was in the bag. Lorenzo would come at Easter, never to return. 'Do you intend to kill him?' Montesecco asked naively. 'Certainly,' the Count replied. 'I want nothing unpleasant to happen to anyone here, but the business must be concluded before his departure.' 'Is our Lord [the Pope] aware of this?' 'Of course he is.' 'By Beelzebub,' exclaimed Montesecco, 'it is providential that he should have given his consent.' 'Don't you realize that he has given us full discretionary power? It is sufficient that our plan should succeed.'

In the event Lorenzo was not tempted by Riario's invitation, and the conspirators reverted to their original scheme. Montesecco issued further instructions to the mercenaries while the Archbishop distributed roles among his agents. By now so many were implicated that there was danger of a leakage. Seven of the ringleaders were assembled in Florence: Jacopo and Francesco de' Pazzi; Archbishop Salviati, who had enlisted the support of his brother Jacopo and a cousin with the same name; Jacopo Bracciolini; and Bernardo Bandini de' Baroncelli.

Bracciolini, a son of the celebrated scholar Poggio, had published an Italian translation of his father's *History of Florence* in 1476, and dedicated his Commentary on Petrarch's *Triumph of Fame* to Lorenzo. He was a member of the Platonic Academy and a friend of Ficino, and considering his fulsome professions of gratitude to Lorenzo in his preface to that Commentary (which was published in 1477 while the conspiracy was in embryo) his defection was remarkably sudden. According to Ammirato, it was due to sheer levity and a craze for novelty, 'forgetting all that his father owed to the Medici, the wealth and renown acquired through their patronage.' Vain, loquacious and malevolent, he had squandered his ample patrimony, and he hoped to recoup himself by offering his services to the Pazzi and Salviati. Recently he had been appointed secretary to Girolamo's nephew, the seventeen-year-old Cardinal Raffaello Riario Sansoni, who had gone to study at Pisa under the Archbishop's guidance. It was easy for the Archbishop to engage Bracciolini in consequence.

The seventh, Bernardo Bandini de' Baroncelli, was a cynical adventurer loaded with debt. Like Bracciolini he hoped to improve his material prospects. Not one of these individuals could be described as an idealist. Girolamo Riario, the spider who had woven the web, crouched prudently in the Roman background. Montesecco was his ambivalent henchman.

Two priests were enlisted at the last moment: Antonio Maffei of Volterra and Stefano da Bagnone. Maffei was a scribe of the Apostolic Chamber who had been deputed by the Pope to convey the cardinal's hat to young Riario Sansoni at Pisa. Poliziano afterwards attributed his complicity to vengeance for the sack of Volterra in 1472. Bagnone was the parish priest of Montemurlo which belonged to the Pazzi; he was also employed as Jacopo's secretary and as tutor to his illegitimate daughter Caterina.

The complicity of other members of the Pazzi family remains questionable. Lorenzo's brother-in-law Guglielmo might have been in the secret, for Poliziano describes him as sitting on both sides of the fence. In his heart of hearts he probably sympathized with his family, and his loud protestations of innocence were not justified by his conduct after the banishment of the Medici. His cousin Renato had held various posts in the government but preferred a life of studious retirement. According to Machiavelli, Renato spoke against the conspiracy at a family reunion, advising his relations to bide their time since Lorenzo's affairs were in such a hopeless muddle that he would be bankrupt within a few years. Having lost wealth and credit, he would lose the State. Let the Pazzi lend him money at high interest and hasten his ruin with slight loss to themselves. But Francesco and Riario were in too great a hurry: Sixtus IV might not last so long.

While Lorenzo's enemies were plotting his murder, he was concerned with the consequences of the murder in Milan. As the Duke's heir was a child, his weak widow, Bona of Savoy, was appointed regent. She now had to contend with her four brothers-in-law, two of whom, Sforza Duke of Bari and Lodovico il Moro, had been banished by her husband. These were reinforced by their brothers Ottaviano and Ascanio, the future Cardinal. The late Duke's prime minister, Cecco Simonetta, tried to protect her against their machinations, and three of them were banished after taking part in an abortive revolt against the government of Milan in Genoa. Ottaviano was drowned in the river Adda during his escape.

Lorenzo was criticized for tolerating Lodovico's presence at Pisa, but he had no wish to antagonize a potential ruler of Milan. Under the Duchess's regency Milan had ceased to be an effective ally. Venice was hardly more serviceable, and King Ferrante of Naples had been estranged by his alliance with the imperious Serenissima.

The general anxiety about events in Lombardy was reflected in Poliziano's correspondence with Lorenzo's mother while she was taking a cure for rheumatism at Bagno a Morba near Volterra. Her rooms there were as dark as an alchemist's, she wrote, and the bugs were as big as capons, but she had faith in the healing effect of the waters. Though she ought to stay on another week to finish the cure, she promised to join her family in Florence for the festivities on St John the Baptist's day.

Her letters to Lorenzo were full of maternal forethought. When he was in Pisa she sent him 'sixteen flasks of good old Greek wine: eight of Poggibonsi marked with ink, and eight of Colle. To us they seem good but you must choose the best, and four *torte besse* [Sienese cakes] besides. I do this because I think you may need them for the visit of Madama [the Duchess of Ferrara] although I suppose you have made every provision. . . . I hope they please you. Do not let the carrier return empty . . .' A fresh supply of oranges and biscuits, she added, would be appreciated.

At the same time Giuliano, who had been suffering from a fever, was taking baths at Corsena near Lucca, which apparently did not hinder his hunting and other sports. He was always prominent in the jousts and football games that enlivened the Carnival season.

Florentine football was more complicated and colourful than our modern game, with twenty-seven players on each side, apart from trumpeters, drummers, standard-bearers, referees, and a ball thrower. Of the twenty-seven players fifteen, divided into three companies, stood facing opponents in the front rank and bore the brunt of the attack. Behind these so-called 'runners' (*corridori*) five 'spoilers' (*sconciatori*), who had to spoil the game for the runners of the opposite side, were scattered across the field. The spoilers were supported by four 'front hitters', and these by three 'back hitters' – or half-backs and backs. The field, usually the square before Santa Croce, was enclosed by a palisade at the top and bottom, by a ditch on the left and a low wall on the right. Stands for the umpires and notabilities were raised along the wall. The referees and standard-bearers of each side, together with brightly uniformed halberdiers at regular intervals, stood round a tent on each side of the field.

Announced by trumpeters and drummers, the players marched to the field in an imposing procession. Selected from the noblest Florentine families, they wore light shoes, long hose, doublet and cap, and their costumes were of velvet, silk, cloth of gold or silver: each side had its own colours. The 'runners' followed in couples, chequer fashion, a red behind a white and *vice versa*. Nine more drummers preceded the standard-bearers, each wearing the colours and bearing the banner of his side. Finally came the 'spoilers', the half-backs carrying the ball, and the backs.

After marching round the field, the procession broke up at the blast of a bugle, and the players took up their positions at regulated distances. The game began after a third trumpet-blast, when the ball was hurled at a marble tablet in the middle of the wall by a man in parti-coloured hose combining the colours of both sides. It rebounded between the 'runners' and those who captured the ball were set upon by the nearest 'spoilers' who tried to pass it to their own 'runners', using their feet, whereas the half-backs and backs were allowed to use their hands. If the runners could get the ball past the spoilers, they had to face a struggle with the half-backs, who might pitch it over the heads of the players to the half-backs on the opposite side. This part of the game was most exciting to the spectators. Having passed the spoilers and half-backs, the runners had to overcome the backs. Usually the ball was knocked, instead of kicked, over the goal, when the two sides changed places, the winners marching to their new position with banner waving, the losers with furled flag and lowered staff. But no diagram could convey the visual kaleidoscope of the game, in which Giuliano was one of the fastest runners.

Poliziano records that he was also a fine dancer and wrestler, for he was 'broad-shouldered, wide chested, with muscular arms, a slim waist, powerful thighs, and shapely legs.' But unlike the average athlete he delighted in music and the arts, and 'he composed good verse in the vernacular'. Devoted to Lorenzo, who had been his mentor since their father's death, he would often join his literary gatherings at Fiesole.

Perched above Florence, misty and golden in the evening light, so pure was the air that it cleared the mind of material dross. To discourse on the contemplative and the active life and visions of a new world was more natural here than in the city below. A green alley vaulted with ilex formed a vista ending in an open space with a fountain where a bevy of girls were listening to a lutanist. He sang a roundelay by Lorenzo in a warm tenor voice and the girls joined the refrain, till the solemn bells of a neighbouring convent chimed and they crossed themselves in silence. Lightly the lutanist kissed their hands and bowed.

He was summoned by the gentlemen in the loggia who were discussing Plato on the refining influence of music. As at Careggi, the number of guests were nine in honour of the nine muses, but other subjects besides Plato and Christian doctrine were debated. Since Poliziano was translating Homer's *Iliad* into Latin hexameters Lorenzo asked him to recite the passage about Helen and Priam watching the Greek army from the walls of Troy.

'Aeons ago yet still vivid, thanks to our Angelo's interpretation. Florence has produced many a Thersites, but I doubt if we have a Pandarus,' Lorenzo remarked.

'There are plenty in Rome, especially in the Vatican, according to hearsay. Homer is indeed less ancient than he seems. History is bound to produce more Helens.'

'Heaven forfend!'

After Poliziano had recited the hexameters describing the rescue of Paris by Aphrodite, the lutanist extemporized a hymn to the goddess. 'We should build a shrine to Homer at Fiesole,' said Lorenzo, 'but Messer Marsilio might not approve. What say you?'

'Our shrine to the blessed Plato should suffice. We know too little about Homer, apart from his blindness. I suspect he had collaborators. But Demetrius Chalcondylas is our best authority on the subject.'

'I wish we could lure him from Padua to Florence. His *editio princeps* ought to be printed here. I have only seen it in manuscript. It is to Greek literature what the *Divine Comedy* is to ours.'

'And what *The Aeneid* is to the Latin ...'

So the great epics and their allegories were compared and analyzed, and the power of poetry prevailed over mundane topics. Lorenzo stimulated the creative ambitions of his companions. He generated heat as well as light. Already Poliziano was meditating his panegyric on Virgil.

In the monastic tranquillity of the Medici villa at Fiesole politics and finance were temporarily shelved. After long days of open-air exercise, and after long nights of love, such conversations were balm to Giuliano's spirit. Lorenzo's guests returned to the city refreshed and renewed.

Giuliano regretted the absence of women at these intellectual feasts, but their presence would have offended Clarice, who had a notion that philosophy was akin to black magic. The little she had heard of Plato repelled her, for how could the love of men for youths lead to higher things? Surely Socrates must have deserved his hemlock. She suspected that the Platonic Academy had an unhealthy influence. That all roads led to Rome was her conviction, and sometimes she wished she had stayed there. Lorenzo's attitude towards the Holy Father distressed her. There was a gleam of mockery in his eyes whenever the Franciscan Pope and his Riario nephews were mentioned: with so many juvenile prelates of dubious pedigree, he could not spare a cardinal's hat for a Medici! Clarice was inwardly relieved that Giuliano remained a layman, for he brought gaiety to Cafaggiolo, and he lightened the gravity of the palace in Via Larga. He was more like a son than a brother to Lorenzo. All attempts by their enemies to separate them had failed.

Having discussed the double murder *ad nauseam*, Count Riario suggested that the Pazzi should invite his nephew, the young Cardinal Raffaello, to Florence. The Medici were obliged to entertain so notable a visitor, which would offer an opportunity for dispatching both brothers. Riario's letters to Lorenzo became even more ingratiating, recommending his artistic nephew, who longed to inspect Lorenzo's famous collection. Having been appointed Papal legate in Perugia, he would pass through Florence on his way from Pisa, when he would stay with Jacopo de' Pazzi at his Montughi villa. In due course a banquet in his honour was prepared at Fiesole. Poliziano brought his pupil Piero, Lorenzo's six-year-old son, to amuse the guests with his prattle, and many notabilities were present. But Giuliano was kept at home by a painful attack of sciatica. Again the conspirators were foiled.

The ride uphill to Fiesole on a sparkling April morning, pausing to admire the view of the city between the olives and cypresses on its grassy slope, was as exhilarating then as it is today. Everybody missed Giuliano, the Pazzi most of all. 'How unfortunate that he was unable to join us!' sighed Franceschino with unusual sincerity.

Lorenzo knew that Franceschino had double-crossed him in the sale of Imola but he let bygones be bygones. After the young Cardinal had mumbled grace in a Latin that Poliziano itched to polish, glasses filled with Trebbiano were raised to the host and his absent brother. 'Long life and better health!' said Jacopo de' Pazzi. 'Blessings, blessings!' added the Cardinal benignly. Franceschino seldom left his side, as if he feared some juvenile indiscretion. 'His Eminence yearns to visit Your Magnificence's treasures,' he told Lorenzo.

'Except for a few illuminated manuscripts they are all in the city.'

'I am more interested in old coins and medals,' said the Cardinal. 'It is a pity that His Holiness parted with those in the late Pope Paul's collection. He is too spiritual to care for worldly things. I'm afraid I am woefully remiss in that respect.'

'The Divine spirit has animated the creators of beauty. I have some old sculpture that is purely pagan, yet its beauty is undeniable.'

'The buried gods and goddesses can be very seductive,' said

Lorenzo. 'I have a marble Venus of Hellenic origin. Her smile is enchanting. As for her bosom . . .'

'You had better not listen to him,' said Franceschino. 'Such talk is too carnal for a Cardinal's ears.'

'We are not in the Vatican yet. While in Florence I must see its masterpieces of art. I may never get another chance . . .'

It was therefore arranged that the Sunday before Ascension Day, which happened to fall on 26 April, Cardinal Raffaello would visit the palace and attend High Mass in the Cathedral. Lorenzo invited His Eminence to a second banquet and the conspirators exulted in anticipation.

Again Giuliano excused himself, for he was still in pain. He hoped, however, to attend Mass. The Pazzi were determined to drag him to the Cathedral, by whatever means. At a final conference they decided that Franceschino and Bandini were to deal with Giuliano, and Montesecco with Lorenzo; but at the last minute the rugged condottiere changed his mind. Nothing could induce him to commit murder in the house of God. The two priests Maffei and Bagnone, who volunteered to replace him, had no such qualms.

The archbishop of Pisa and his retinue were to capture the Palace of the Signoria while old Jacopo de' Pazzi was to rouse the populace. The defection of Montesecco was disappointing but at least he was obliged to direct military operations.

On Sunday Cardinal Raffaello and his suite rode into the city from Montughi. Lorenzo awaited him outside the Cathedral, but was told that he had gone to the Medici palace to don his ecclesiastical vestments. So Lorenzo went back to meet him at the foot of the staircase and together they walked to the Duomo. The archbishop of Florence and all the canons escorted the boyish Cardinal with pomp and incense to the high altar while the organ pealed a Gregorian paean.

'*In nomine Patris, et Filii, et Spiritus Sancti. Amen.*' The congregation was enormous, swelled by the conspirators with their horde of armed retainers. Lorenzo joined a group of friends in the passage round the choir.

'*Introibo ad altare Dei* . . .' During the antiphon Franceschino and Bandini searched for Giuliano. Where the devil was he? This time they could not let him slip through their fingers. They rushed to the palace where they found him resting on a couch. He complained of his aching leg. 'Consider your immortal soul,' said Franceschino with smiling unction. 'Your absence will grieve His Eminence. For the sake of our honoured guest from Rome I implore you to make a supreme effort. Between the two of us we can help you on the way. We could even carry you, if necessary.'

Giuliano was not easy to persuade. As if to support him, but in fact to ascertain if he were protected by a corselet, they hugged him as they sauntered on the Via Larga, arm in arm. 'You're getting as plump as a partridge,' said Bandini facetiously. 'I'm sure all the girls will be looking for you in the Duomo.' His joviality was somewhat forced while he was pondering where to deliver the first blow. Usually Giuliano wore a hunting knife in his belt, but as it chafed his thigh he was totally disarmed. Franceschino and Bandini stood close to him near the chapel of the Holy Cross, whereas Lorenzo was on the other side of the choir. The Paternoster had been recited and the congregation were kneeling before the Blessed Sacrament. '*Agnus Dei, qui tollis peccata mundi: miserere nobis.*'

No two witnesses concur about the precise moment when Giuliano was attacked but it was probably when the bell tinkled for the Elevation of the Host. More than four centuries later when his tomb was opened, a deep sword cut was visible in the top of his skull; it had evidently been delivered while he was in a bending position. According to some, Giuliano was struck between the priest's Communion and *Ite missa est*, when the congregation began to disperse. Poliziano wrote that Bandini plunged a short dagger into Giuliano's chest and that Franceschino continued to strike him repeatedly after he had fallen: nineteen wounds were counted in his corpse. Giuliano's servants scampered behind the altar without attempting to defend him; all those in his vicinity scrambled for the nearest door.

On the opposite side near the old sacristy and the altar of St Zenobius, the two priests Maffei and Bagnone, with a band of Jacopo de' Pazzi's bravoes and some Spaniards of the Cardinal's suite, were stealing towards Lorenzo. Maffei put a hand on Lorenzo's shoulder, expecting him to turn so that he could stab him in the throat or chest. But Lorenzo promptly whirled his cloak round his left arm and drew his sword; the priest's dagger merely inflicted a light wound in his neck. As Lorenzo leapt through the choir and across the high altar, Franceschino and Bandini tried to intercept him, but his old friend, Francesco Nori, and other stalwarts barred the way. Nori was killed outright by a thrust in the stomach; Lorenzino Cavalcanti was wounded in an arm; and it is more likely that Franceschino's leg was wounded in the scuffle than that it was gashed in the fury of his assault on Giuliano.

Lorenzo reached the northern sacristy, where Poliziano and his companions fastened the bronze door.

The two priests had escaped, and it was the turn of Bandini and Franceschino to slip away. Few members of the congregation realized what had happened. There was a frantic stampede and much shouting from those who imagined that Brunelleschi's dome had collapsed. At first Lorenzo and his friends in the sacristy could not tell if the building had been invaded by their foes. Fearing that Maffei's dagger had been poisoned, Antonio Ridolfi insisted on sucking the wound in Lorenzo's neck. Lorenzo kept asking: 'Is Giuliano safe?' – but nobody could answer. All were in an agony of suspense.

Sigismondo della Stufa climbed into the organ loft. He could see the mangled corpse of Giuliano in a pool of blood below and could hear Lorenzo's Pazzi brother-in-law hysterically protesting his innocence.

Once it was ascertained that the few people left in the Cathedral were partisans, the bronze door was opened and Lorenzo was escorted home, his friends forming a phalanx to spare him the sight of his murdered brother.

The canons of the Cathedral looked after the terrified young Cardinal who knelt trembling beside the altar, till two members of the Eight (police) and a squad of soldiers hustled him to the town hall, for he was in danger of being lynched by the mob. Old and young, priests and laymen, had taken up arms to defend the Medici, whose palace was surrounded by citizens anxious for their safety. They clamoured for the blood of Lorenzo's enemies. An hour later he addressed them from a balcony. His neck was bandaged and he was deathly pale. But his voice was loud and calm. 'My people, I commend myself to you. Control yourselves and let justice take its course. Do not harm the innocent. My wound is not serious . . .'

His speech was drowned in deafening acclamations. The loyalty of the crowd was a promising grain of comfort. Lorenzo now stood alone, and alone he resolved to stand for Florence, whatever might happen. And whatever enemies lurked beyond his territory, the Florentines were his friends. Giuliano had been their idol and they thirsted for vengeance.

Pretending that he had to visit his ailing mother, Archbishop Salviati had left the Cathedral with a group of accomplices who were joined by an armed band of some thirty Perugian exiles. His intention was to seize the Palace of the Signoria. Some of these ruffians loitered below, others followed him up the stairs and hid in the secretarial office to await his signal. The priors were at dinner when the Archbishop sent word that he had come with a personal message from the Pope. Nobody likes his dinner to be interrupted and Cesare Petrucci, the gonfalonier, replied that he would meet Salviati in an anteroom.

Remembering the abortive rebellion at Prato, Petrucci's suspicion was roused by this impromptu visit. Salviati's relations stood outside with Jacopo Bracciolini while the prelate told Petrucci that the Pope intended to promote his son in Rome. His manner was strangely hesitant: he coughed and stammered and his speech became incoherent as he peered nervously towards the door. As soon as Petrucci summoned the guard the Archbishop dashed out of the room calling for his retainers. Petrucci pursued him, colliding with Bracciolini whom he seized by the hair and knocked down in a scuffle. The Perugians were trapped, for the door they had closed was fitted with a spring bolt. After consigning Bracciolini to the guard, Petrucci and the priors, seizing a roasting spit and other extempore weapons, climbed the high tower and fastened it with a heavy chain. The doors on the public square were bolted; the Archbishop and his accomplices were arrested. The tocsin was tolled to warn the citizens, who rushed to the palace fully armed.

Jacopo de' Pazzi rode through the crowd with a hundred retainers shouting 'People and Liberty!' But the people only booed and cursed him with cries of 'Down with the traitors! *Palle, Palle!*' (balls, the arms of the Medici). So many stones were thrown down on him from the palace tower that he was forced to retreat. Furtively he reached his own dwelling, where Franceschino lay concealed – prostrated by the wound in his thigh. Jacopo still hoped that the papal troops would save the situation, but when none arrived after several hours he rode to the Santa Croce gate which was guarded by Montesecco with a band of mercenaries. Montesecco had come the same morning with thirty mounted crossbowmen and fifty infantry from Imola under the pretext of escorting Cardinal Raffaello to Perugia, but many of these had already been massacred by the mob. Since Jacopo and his nephew Andrea could only think of flight, Montesecco accompanied them in the direction of the Mugello.

As soon as the priors were informed of Giuliano's murder the Perugians trapped in the secretary's office were slaughtered and hurled into the square. Franceschino was pulled naked and bleeding from his hiding place and hanged from a window of the city palace. The archbishop of Pisa was hanged beside him and as he fell, he bit at the dead body of Franceschino; the halter tightening round his throat, he held on to the corpse with his teeth. On the following day, 27th April, the two other Salviati were strangled before they were hanged at various windows with other members of the Archbishop's staff. Jacopo Bracciolini shared the same fate. Soon the windows of the palaces of the Signoria and of the Podestà, or chief of police, were festooned with dangling corpses. Those who were not hanged were despoiled, hacked to pieces and dragged through the streets, their heads sawn off and exhibited on pikes. Students of the pathology of mob violence would have enjoyed a succession of field days as the sanguinary contagion spread, regardless of Lorenzo's exhortations. Many a severed limb was used in childish games; some hearts and livers found their way into the cooking pot. Ears and noses were sliced off, eyes scooped out of their sockets. There was a free-for-all orgy of mutilation and agonized shrieks swelled the chorus of raucous vengeance. The hunt for fugitives provided fiendish sport. It was lucky for Cardinal Raffaello that he was guarded as a hostage.

The innocent suffered with the guilty. Renato de' Pazzi, who had argued against the conspiracy, escaped from his country house in peasant's disguise but he was recognized, arrested, and hanged ignominiously. His brothers, who were just as innocent, were immured in the dungeons of Volterra. Lorenzo's brother-in-law Guglielmo sought refuge in the Medici palace. His wife Bianca pleaded for him though he too was under suspicion. For his own safety he was banished within twenty miles of Florence. While Bianca stayed behind with the children, he prudently retired to Rome till the storm blew over.

The papal troops from Imola and Città di Castello who had crossed the frontier were withdrawn when the failure of the conspiracy was reported. Bernardo Bandini, who had struck the first blow, was one of the last to be captured. He contrived to escape as far as Constantinople on a Neapolitan galley. A year later he was arrested by Sultan Mohammed II and extradited at the request of the Florentine ambassador Antonio de' Medici, a cousin of Lorenzo. He was hanged in his Turkish costume from a window of the Bargello, an exotic advertisement of the long arm of the law. A macabre record of the event has been left in a drawing by Leonardo da Vinci, now in the Musée Bonnat at Bayonne. As Miss Eve Borsook has observed,* 'it was really the dress that interested him and he carefully jotted down the details beside the drawing: "Tawny cap; black satin vest; black sleeveless coat lined; a turquoise blue jacket lined with fox; and the collar of the jacket appliquéd with black and red velvet; Bernardo di Bandini Baroncigli; black hose."'

Old Jacopo, laird of the Pazzi clan, was captured by peasants on his way to the Romagna. Aware of what was in store for him, he offered them gold if they would kill him on the spot. One dealt him such a crippling blow that he had to be carried to Florence on a litter. He was ready enough to confess without the excruciating preliminaries. A lifelong gambler, he said he had counted on the luck of Franceschino whose investments on behalf of the Pope had invariably been successful. 'Why did you fail to consider the superior luck of Lorenzo?' his examiner retorted. He was hanged from the same window as the Archbishop in a purple gown and stockings, his hands tied behind him with a leather strap. Cursing and blaspheming until his last breath, he consigned his soul to the devil.

His posthumous peregrinations were related in Luca Landucci's diary. It is unlikely that he was buried in the family chapel designed by Brunelleschi as its exterior was still unfinished in 1478. Owing to weird nocturnal noises and a persistent rainfall which threatened the crops, the people supposed that they were being punished by Heaven

* *Companion Guide to Florence*, London 1966.

for allowing a murderous blasphemer to be buried in consecrated ground.

On 15 May Landucci wrote that 'the body of Messer Jacopo was disinterred in Santa Croce and buried near the city wall, whereupon the weather cleared,' and on 17 May: 'At about 20 in the evening [4 p.m.] some boys disinterred it a second time, and dragged it through Florence by the piece of rope that was still round its neck; and when they reached the door of his house they tied the rope to the door-bell, saying "Knock at the door!" and they made great sport all over the town. And when they grew tired and did not know what more to do with it, they went to the Rubiconte bridge and cast it in the river. And they sang a ditty with certain rhymes like:

> Messer Jacopo is floating
> Down the Arno past the boating.

And it was considered an extraordinary thing, first because children are usually afraid of dead bodies, and secondly because the stench was so nauseous that it was impossible to go near it; imagine what it was like from the 27th April till the 17th May! They must have had to touch it with their hands to throw it into the Arno. As it floated down the river, always keeping above the surface, the bridges were crowded with people to watch it pass. And another day, down towards Brozzi, the boys pulled it out of the water again and hung it on a willow; then they beat it and threw it back into the Arno. They say it was seen to pass under the bridges of Pisa, always above the surface.'

The people were more amused than horrified by these antics, and their latent cruelty found many an outlet in these homicidal eruptions. Lorenzo's partisans were *plus royalistes que le roi* and he was unable to curb their zeal. The executions dragged on long after Giuliano's burial in San Lorenzo on 30 April (Ascension Day), when a vast concourse of mourning citizens, with weapons under their cloaks, attended his funeral. Machiavelli – no partisan of the Medici – wrote that Giuliano was accompanied 'with the tears of all citizens because of his liberality and humanity.' He was only twenty-four.

It is not certain when the condottiere Montesecco was captured but he was examined, probably with additional torture, on 4 May, and his written confession is our main source of information about the conspiracy. A soldier of fortune doomed shortly to die, he had nothing left to conceal. The document was signed and witnessed by the chief of police and five friars before he was beheaded in the courtyard of the Bargello, at that time the palace of the Podestà. On the same day the two priests who had wounded Lorenzo were hanged after their noses and ears were cut off. They had been hiding in the monastery of the Badia, whose friars barely escaped the same penalty.

Cardinal Raffaello Riario was held as a hostage from 26 April till 5 June. After Montesecco's confession the Signoria became convinced of his innocence, but while he remained in Florence the Pope was less likely to persecute the colony of Florentine merchants and bankers in Rome. Appeals from Venice, Naples and Rome for his release induced the Signoria to set him free. In a letter to the Pope the Cardinal stated that Lorenzo and the government had treated him with the utmost consideration and begged His Holiness to relent. But Sixtus was inflexible.

Altogether about a hundred suspects were executed and the Florentine ringleaders were depicted by Botticelli on the walls of the Palace of the Signoria and of the Bargello. Vasari, who erroneously attributed the paintings to Andrea del Castagno, described them (evidently from hearsay) as 'a perfect wonder ... Verily it would not be possible adequately to describe the art and judgment displayed in these figures, for the most part copied from the life and hung up by the feet in the strangest attitudes, which were infinitely varied and exceedingly fine.' In fact, figures represented as hanging by one foot denoted that they had been outlawed, not executed. Herbert Horne has proved that 'within the space of some twelve weeks Botticelli's frescoes were commissioned, executed, and paid 40 gold florins for on 21st July, 1478.' Lorenzo himself made the epitaphs under these figures, 'and among the rest, the one for Bernardo Bandini, which ran in this wise:

Son Bernardo Bandini un nuovo Giuda,
Traditore micidiale in chiesa io fui,
Ribello per aspettare morte più cruda.'

('I am Bernardo Bandini, another Judas. A murderous traitor in church was I. A rebel awaiting more cruelly to die.' – i.e. a more cruel death than that he had inflicted on Giuliano.) The subject, wrote Horne, 'must have especially commended itself to the virile genius of Botticelli,' hence the loss of these frescoes 'cannot be sufficiently deplored.'*

Bandini and Franzesi were still at large while the artist was thus employed. Franzesi's role in the plot was uncertain, but it is known that he was helped to escape by Pietro Vespucci, a former captain general of the Florentine galleys and envoy to Naples. Vespucci was arrested on 1 May and condemned to the Stinche, the common prison, on the 7th. He had been openly pro-Pazzi at the time of Giuliano's murder. Then, seeing the way the wind blew, he urged the mob to set fire to the Pazzi palace, which was prevented by Piero Corsini. His belated zeal on both sides aroused suspicion. Like others who had joined the Pazzi he was in financial straits and hoped to benefit by a change of régime. It was said that he nursed a grudge against Giuliano on account of his sentimental attachment to Simonetta Cattaneo, the wife of his son Marco, but this is improbable since Marco had remarried in 1477 after Simonetta's death. Lorenzo had been on cordial terms with the Vespucci and sent his own doctor to attend Simonetta during her fatal decline. Now Marco was exiled.

---

* Herbert P. Horne: *Sandro Botticelli, Painter of Florence*, London 1908.

On 23 May the new gonfalonier, Giacomo degli Alessandri, and the priors decreed that the Pazzi coat of arms was to be removed or destroyed.

Their property was confiscated, and all Jacopo's stables, clothes and household effects were sold at auction. Whoever married a descendant of Andrea de' Pazzi was to lose his right to hold office in Florence, and violators of this rule were to be fined, punished and declared rebels. That the dolphin arms on the Pazzi palace in Via del Proconsolo are still *in situ* shows that the rule was not observed too strictly. Eventually the surviving Pazzi were amnestied. Vespucci was set free in 1480 and Guglielmo returned from exile in 1482.

Vasari informs us that 'it was ordained by the friends and relations of Lorenzo that many figures of him should be set up in various places as a thanksgiving to God for his safety. Orsini, among others, with the help of Andrea Verrocchio, made three life-size figures in wax, carving the skeleton in wood ... and completing it with split canes. The framework was then covered with waxed cloth, folded and arranged with so much beauty and elegance that nothing better or more true to nature could be seen. The heads, hands, and feet were afterwards made of thicker wax but hollow inside; the features were copied from life, and the whole was painted in oil with such ornaments and additions of the hair and other details as were required, all which being entirely natural and perfectly executed, no longer appeared to be figures in wax, but living men. . . . One of these is in the church which belongs to the Nuns of Chiarito in the Via di San Gallo ... and is clothed in the habiliments worn by Lorenzo when, wounded in the neck and with that part bandaged, he showed himself at a window of his palace to the people, who had rushed there to see if he were alive, as they hoped, or to avenge him if he were dead. The second figure of Lorenzo is clad in the *lucco* which is the ordinary robe of Florentine citizens, and this is in the church of the Servites, the SS. Annunziata. . . . The third was sent to Assisi for the church of Santa Maria degli Angeli.'

Unfortunately these figures have gone the way of Botticelli's portraits of the conspirators. Only the fine medal to commemorate the tragedy still exists, with profiles of Lorenzo (*Salus publica*) and Giuliano (*Luctus publicus*) above the cathedral choir, and the scene of violence below.

Discovering that Giuliano had left an illegitimate son christened Giulio, only a few months old, Lorenzo had him educated with his own children. Leo X legitimized him and made him a Cardinal. Eventually he became Pope Clement VII.

20, 21 The Medici (above) and Pazzi (below) coats of arms, displaying the familiar *palle* (balls) and the bellicose dolphins.

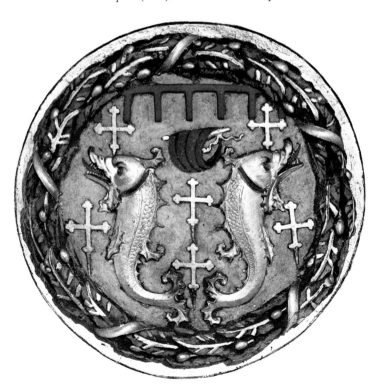

22 Pope Sixtus IV giving audience to the humanist Platina, who became Keeper
of the Vatican Library; a fresco by Melozzo da Forlì. The four standing figures
are the Pope's ambitious nephews: from left to right are Giovanni della Rovere,
Girolamo Riario, Giuliano della Rovere and Pietro Riario. Girolamo was one of
the prime movers of the Pazzi Conspiracy.

23 Federigo da Montefeltro, Duke of Urbino; portrait by Piero della Francesca.
At first an ally of the Medici, Federigo was won over by the Pope and his aides.

24, 25 Galeazzo Maria Sforza, the dissolute Duke of Milan after the death of his father Francesco in 1466 (see ill. 4), was himself assassinated in a church in Milan in 1476. The woodcut of 1505 (above) gives an impression of the event, which was meant to be a gesture against Sforza's tyrannous government.

26 A view of the Florence Duomo from above shows the altar before which
Giuliano de' Medici was attacked and killed by the conspirators, Bernardo
Bandini de' Baroncelli and Franceschino de' Pazzi. On the opposite side of the
church Lorenzo was able to resist the attempt made on his life.

27, 28 A medal was struck, not long after the event, to commemorate the Pazzi
Conspiracy and its failure to exterminate Medici power in Florence. On the one
side of the coin (above) is the survivor, Lorenzo, on the other the popular 24-
year-old victim, Giuliano.

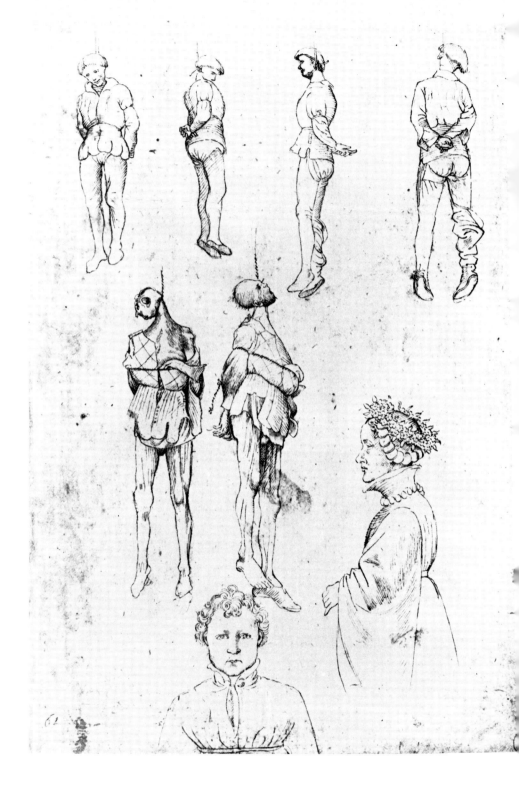

29 Studies by Pisanello
(c. 1397–1455) of hanged
men give some impression of
the orgy of revenge which
took place in Florence and
neighbouring cities following
the Pazzi Conspiracy.

30 The drawing by Leonardo
da Vinci (right) is of the
assassin Bandini de' Baroncelli,
who escaped to Constantinople
but was recaptured and hanged
from a window of the Bargello.

31–34 Four of the Medici villas
outside Florence. Top left, Il
Trebbio, an early building on
top of a hill in the Mugello, that
area from which the Medici
originally stemmed. Left, the
façade of Poggio a Caiano,
which Lorenzo had rebuilt for
him by Giuliano da Sangallo
1480–85. Above, Cafaggiolo,
which was built for Cosimo by
Michelozzo not far from Il
Trebbio. Careggi, right, the first
of the Medici country dwellings,
was particularly dear to Cosimo,
who went there frequently for
relaxation. It was at Careggi that
the Platonic Academy was
founded at the beginning of
Lorenzo's tenancy.

35, 36 Frescoes by Domenico Ghirlandaio in the Sassetti Chapel in Santa
Trinità, Florence, introduce members of the Medici family into religious scenes.
Left, Poliziano with Lorenzo's son, Piero, in a detail from the fresco depicting
the confirmation of the rule of St Francis. The detail above shows Lorenzo
himself between Francesco Sassetti on his right and Antonio Pucci on his left.

37 The Raphael portrait of the first Medici pope, Leo X (Lorenzo's son Giovanni), with Cardinal Giulio (Giuliano's illegitimate son, later Pope Clement VII) and Luigi de' Rossi.

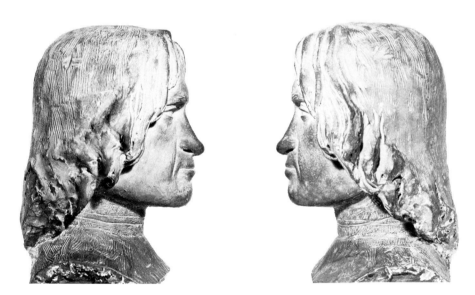

38 Three views of a bust of Lorenzo the Magnificent, made only a few years after his death in 1492.

39 *Overleaf:* Lorenzo's death mask.

4

WAR WITH THE PAPACY
AND NAPLES

*Lorenzo's visit to Naples: a diplomatic
triumph*

N EWS of the Pazzi conspiracy spread throughout Europe as swiftly as if the telephone had already been invented. Within a short time Lorenzo was receiving the condolences of foreign potentates and allies. Politically his situation was the reverse of what the conspirators had hoped for. His power had been consolidated.

The Pope's first impulse was to deplore Giuliano's murder in an official letter to the Signoria, but his inward fury and frustration were lashed to a frenzy by Girolamo Riario. The summary execution of an archbishop and other priests while his great nephew Cardinal Raffaello was kept as a hostage seemed far more sacrilegious than the murder of Giuliano in the Cathedral. Count Riario's reaction was to seize the old Florentine ambassador, Donato Acciaiuoli, and consign him to the Castle of St Angelo, but the intervention of the Venetian and Milanese ambassadors, who announced that they would join him, deterred the Pope from perpetrating this outrage. Acciaiuoli protested with such vehemence that Sixtus allowed him to return to his residence, denying responsibility for Riario's conduct. Other Florentines who had been arrested were released for fear of reprisals while the young Cardinal was still in Florence.

Sixtus now hoped to separate Lorenzo from his people by publishing a bull of excommunication against him as a 'son of iniquity and offspring of perdition,' studiously avoiding any reference to the conspiracy. Next he fulminated an interdict against Florence, Pisa and

Pistoia, unless Lorenzo and his guilty associates in the government were surrendered for condign punishment. All their property was to go to the Church, their houses to be levelled to the ground: 'let eternal ruin witness their eternal disgrace.' King Ferrante of Naples, as the Pope's ally, also demanded the expulsion of Lorenzo.

The Florentine Signoria rejected these demands with irony and indignation. War was the inevitable consequence: in July Neapolitan troops under Alfonso, Duke of Calabria, Ferrante's eldest son, were camping near Montepulciano. Though Cardinal Raffaello had been released on 5 July and had left Florence a week later, Sixtus recapitulated all his grievances and enforced his interdict with greater severity. The Signoria replied that Lorenzo had been the staunch defender of their liberties, emphasizing their right to manage their own affairs. His safety was the guarantee of theirs, for which they were ready to sacrifice everything. They urged the Pope to remember his holy office as the Vicar of Christ and reminded him that the King of France was their patron and protector.

Louis XI had sent the Signoria an eloquent letter of condolence, to be followed by his special envoy Philippe de Comines (Commynes) and a protest to the Pope. 'God is my witness', Lorenzo wrote to Louis on 19 June, 'that I have committed no crime against the Pope, save that I am alive ... and have not allowed myself to be murdered. This is my sin, for this alone have I been excommunicated and attacked. But I believe that God, scrutinizer of hearts and most just Judge, who knows my innocence, will not permit this and will defend me, whom He saved from those sacrilegious hands in front of His Body, from such impious calumny. On our side we have Canon Law, on our side laws natural and political, on our side truth and innocence, on our side God and mankind. He has violated all these at once, and now desires to annihilate us. I write these things to Your Majesty as to a compassionate father, and from you, on account of your goodness, piety, and greatness of soul, I have no doubt I shall receive much help, favour, and military aid, if required. For we cannot believe that any good man could tolerate that he, who wilfully plunges into such an abyss of crime, should drag along with him the Christian name.' (19 June 1478)

Unfortunately for Lorenzo, King Louis could offer him only moral support. Venice was too embroiled with the Turks and Milan, too weakened by internal dissensions, to assist Florence against the Papal-Neapolitan invasion. Both sides suffered from the common handicap of mercenaries but Lorenzo's disadvantage was that they fought on Tuscan soil, with more pillage and destruction than fighting. Machiavelli has stigmatized the mercenaries as useless and dangerous, 'disunited, undisciplined, unfaithful, valiant before friends, cowardly before enemies.... They have no other reason for keeping the field than a trifle of stipend, which is not enough to induce them to risk their lives for you. They are quite ready to be your soldiers while you do not wage war, but if war comes they take themselves off or run from the foe ...'

When the Pope's ultimatum arrived with the Duke of Calabria's trumpet, Lorenzo rose magnificently to the occasion. He delivered a moving speech to an assembly of leading citizens in the Palace of the Signoria, expressing his gratitude for their loyal protection and his deep regret that he should be unwittingly a cause of conflict to the city he loved more than life. His own conscience was clear: he hoped that Providence would deliver the people from their present predicament, but if they considered that his death or exile would serve the public weal, he freely offered his life, his property, the blood of his children, to his country. His audience responded with a unanimous ovation: his duty was to stand by the republic.

The popular festival of St John the Baptist had been postponed by the general mourning for Giuliano: instead of 24 June it was celebrated on 5 July to bolster up the public morale with pageantry and games in spite of the emergency.

A shop-front dressing competition was held on St John's eve, when the merchants of every guild vied in the tasteful exhibition of their wares, brocades and silks, cloths of gold and silver, jewellery and pearl ornaments, plate and precious vessels of various kinds – a sight calculated to impress outsiders with the prosperity of Medicean Florence.

The guilds also contributed some ingenious novelty to the morrow's ceremony. At noon the clergy in their richest robes carried relics of the saints in a procession through the city, followed by personifications of saints and angels, accompanied by music. Later, when the temperature cooled, an immense torch, offered by the directors of the Mint, was borne on a chariot drawn by two oxen with decorative harness, followed by 400 citizens belonging to the guild of moneychangers. The chariot was 43 feet high, divided into four compartments, diminishing in size towards the apex. The lowest contained three niches on each side, within four of which stood figures in ecclesiastical garb and a child representing the infant Baptist in the centre. The second compartment contained four more boys in white, holding a shield with the arms of the priors on one side and of the Mint on the other. A statue of St John crowned the summit. The priors and leading officials of the republic wound up the procession with a large retinue to the sound of drums and fifes, and the horses which were to run for the *palio* (the prize of red velvet or silk, lined with grey miniver and trimmed with ermine) were led into church to be blessed. The *palio*, drawn by another chariot, was displayed at the winning post, and the race was run from the eastern Porta alla Croce to the western Porta al Prato.

A hundred *edifizi* (towers mounted on carts) were placed round the Piazza della Signoria as symbols of the tribute paid by towns subject to Florence. These were made of wood, cardboard or wax brightly painted, with figures in relief representing scriptural and mythological subjects, men prancing on steeds, others on foot armed with lances and shields, dancing girls, animals, trees and fruit. The towers were kept revolving to display their variety of design. A hundred *palii* of silk or velvet hung from the iron rings on the façade of the town hall.

Landucci in his diary also mentions '*girandole, spiritegli* and *giganti* and many fine things, as if it had been the real St John's day.' These were platforms piled with rockets and ingenious fireworks; men on stilts moving 'like spirits of the air' amid the dense throng, and others disguised as giants with grotesque masks supported on high poles. Many marriages were celebrated on St John's day, which was usually devoted to music, song and dancing.

It was a momentary illusion of peace and plenty while the Papal-Neapolitan troops were advancing towards the frontier. Lorenzo sent his wife and children to Pistoia, where they stayed as guests of the Panciatichi family. Poliziano had to accompany them as tutor to Piero, Lorenzo's eldest son, an obstreperous child of seven. For the sensitive scholar-poet, accustomed to the society of erudite humanists, this was a period of purgatory. Clarice, already suffering from tuberculosis, could not conceal her antipathy. Tuscan wit was wasted on this haughty Roman matron. Everybody's nerves were frayed since the murder of Giuliano and its grisly sequel. An outbreak of plague added to their alarms. 'I get all the kicks,' Poliziano wrote to Lorenzo. 'I am longing for news that the plague has ceased on account of my anxiety for you and in order to return to your service, for I hoped and expected to join you, but since you, or rather my ill fortune, assigned me to this post I endure it, though it requires considerable patience.' 'We want for nothing,' he wrote again on 26 August, 'only we grieve sorely over your trials, which indeed are considerable . . . Be of good cheer and take courage, for great men are moulded by adversity.'

In October they moved from green and gracious Pistoia to the grey fortress-villa of Cafaggiolo in the Mugello, where Poliziano's spirits sank to their nadir. On 18 December he wrote to Lorenzo: 'I remain indoors by the fireside in slippers and a great coat; were you to see me you would think I was melancholy personified. Perhaps I am but myself after all, for I neither do, nor see, nor hear anything that gives me pleasure, so much have I taken our calamities to heart. Sleeping and waking they haunt me. Two days ago we began to spread our wings for we heard the plague had ceased; now we are again depressed on learning that it still persists. When at Florence we have some sort of satisfaction, if nought else that of seeing Lorenzo come home in safety. Here we are in perpetual anxiety about everything. As for myself I declare to you that I am drowned in weary sloth, such is my solitude. I say solitude because Monsignore [probably Gentile Becchi, Bishop of Arezzo] shuts himself up in his room with only his thoughts for company, and I always find him so full of sorrow and dread that my melancholy is only increased in his company. . . . When I am tired of study I ring the changes on plague and war, on grief for the past and fear for the future, and have nobody with whom to air my fantasies. I do not find my Lady Lucrezia with whom I could unburden myself and I am bored to death. . . . However, I try to arm myself with hope and cling to every ray of it in order not to sink to the bottom.'

Tempers collided amid the damp discomfort of their comparative isolation, and Clarice dismissed Poliziano after a final dispute. Much to her annoyance Lorenzo winked at the moody poet's peccadillos. On 28 May 1479, while still at Cafaggiolo, she complained to him: 'I should be glad not to be turned into ridicule by Franco, as was Luigi Pulci, and also that Messer Agnolo [Poliziano] should not be able to boast that he will live in your house whether I like it or not, and that you have put him into your own room at Fiesole. You know I told you that if you wished him to remain I was quite content, and although I have endured a thousand insults, if it has been by your permission I will be patient, but this I can hardly believe . . .'

Little Piero continued to beg his father to send him a pony, 'for I think of it night and day, and until the pony comes I shall have no peace.' When it arrived Piero thanked him profusely for so handsome a gift and promised: 'I shall try and repay you by becoming what you wish. . . . I shall try with all my heart.'

When there was a case of plague at Cafaggiolo the family moved to the more ancient and solitary castle of Il Trebbio some distance above it, where at least the children seem to have been healthy and happy.

Though the Pope's interdict was treated as invalid, the plague and increased taxation added to the people's distress. Unfortunately Lorenzo entrusted the command of his mercenaries to Ercole d'Este, Duke of Ferrara, an incompetent general of dubious loyalty since he was a son-in-law of the King of Naples and brother-in-law of the Duke of Calabria, who led the Neapolitan troops. He relied on an astrologer for his tactics as some now rely on a psychoanalyst. After accepting the baton of command in August he would not budge till 27 September when the stars were presumed to be propitious. His allies were of scant assistance, whereas the Papal troops were commanded by Federigo of Urbino, to whom Sixtus wrote on 25 July 1478: 'We trust that God, whose honour and glory are at stake, will grant you victory in everything, especially as our intentions are straightforward and just. For we make war on no one save that ungrateful, excommunicated and heretical Lorenzo de' Medici, and we pray to God to punish him for his infamous acts, and to you as God's minister deputed to avenge the wrongs he has iniquitously and without cause committed against God and His Church, with such ingratitude that the fountain of infinite love has been dried up.'

Sixtus closed his eyes to the misdeeds of his nephew Girolamo. The latter had sent a secret agent to Florence to compromise Lorenzo with plausible accusations. On 18 June Antonio Pucci wrote to Lorenzo at Cafaggiolo: 'That priest from Imola has been interrogated. He says Count Girolamo sent him here to offer, under the pretext that he had been maltreated, to poison the Count; presuming that we, desiring the Count's death, would provide him with the venom. We were then to be accused to the Pope, and in the Consistory, and the Count was to show the venom, saying, "Look, Lorenzo de' Medici has attempted to poison me." He also offered to consign into our hands one of the gates of Imola in order to accuse us before the Pope and the Cardinals so that they might imagine that we were going to make war on the Pope. He has been tortured and shall be put to the question again in order to get everything out of him.'

Under so inept a commander as Ercole d'Este the Tuscan troops would have been overwhelmed had there not been mercenaries of the same kidney on the opposite side. De Comines, the French envoy, was amazed that the Florentines were not obliterated. Quarrels among their captains as among their mongrel troops over booty; the traditional truce on the approach of winter; futile appeals to Venice and Milan for more active support; diversions in Umbria; plots at Pistoia; anti-Florentine tumults at Lucca – the war was disastrous for Florence and for Lorenzo.

Luca Landucci, the apothecary whose comments were characteristic of his class, wrote in his diary: 'The rule for our Italian soldiers seems to be this: "You pillage there, and we will pillage here; there is no need for us to approach too close to one another." They often let a fort be bombarded for several days, without attempting to succour it. We require to be taught by the northern soldiers how to make war.' In September seven or eight citizens were dying every day of the plague, which began to spread among the troops, and by Christmas, 'what with the terror of the war, the plague, and the Papal interdict, the citizens were in sorry plight. They lived in constant dread, and no one had any heart to work . . . all classes suffered.'

Failing military support, Louis XI of France tried to help Lorenzo by diplomatic means. His appeal to Sixtus for the union of Christendom against the Turks and for arbitration in the dispute with Lorenzo only caused the Pope to repeat his stipulation that Lorenzo should 'confess his guilt and submit to condign punishment'. Louis threatened him with a General Council to reform the Church and forbade the export of bullion to Rome, but Sixtus remained inflexible and the war continued. In 1479, during the second campaign, the Florentines were heavily defeated at Poggio Imperiale near Poggibonsi.

Instead of advancing, however, the Duke of Calabria besieged Colle di Val d'Elsa, only thirty miles from Florence, for two months. Though Colle fell in November, the Neapolitan troops were demoralized by the vigorous defence and Federigo of Urbino, their ablest commander, was taken ill. A three months' truce was welcomed by the battered Florentines.

Having heard from his envoy to Milan that the King of Naples would be willing to negotiate with him privately, Lorenzo bravely decided to risk a conference with the less virulent of his enemies. King Ferrante was a bloodthirsty ogre, but he had a civilized entourage and he wished to gain a reputation for culture. His younger son, Federigo, and his daughter-in-law the Duchess of Calabria appreciated Lorenzo's qualities, and the King's chief counsellor Diomede Carafa, Count of Maddaloni, was well disposed towards him. Among Florentines Filippo Strozzi was most familiar with the Neapolitan court, so Lorenzo sent him on a secret mission in November, as he related in his diary: 'I was to inform the King that Lorenzo placed himself in his hands, and would willingly do all the King desired if he only gave peace to Florence and restored to her the towns she had lost. I found His Majesty at Arnone hunting, and when I delivered my message he answered that he had later news; that Lorenzo was coming in person, and so we would wait and see what his visit would bring forth.'

Lorenzo had summoned some forty leading citizens and announced his intention to go to Naples but the date of his departure was not divulged. Secrecy had always been one of his characteristics and it grew upon him towards middle age. As a Ferrarese ambassador was to write: 'The Magnificent Lorenzo is a man who does not waste many words, and tells his intentions to no one until he is sure of obtaining what he wants. He never says four until he has it safe in a sack.'

He chose Tommaso Soderini to deputize for him during his absence and wrote to the Signoria from San Miniato al Tedesco on 7 December

1479, explaining that he had not notified them of the reasons for his departure because 'in the dangerous circumstances in which our city is placed it was more necessary to act than to deliberate. . . . I therefore propose, with your permission, to proceed directly to Naples. Being the person most hated and persecuted by our enemies I may, by delivering myself into their hands, be the means of restoring peace to our city.' He made it clear that, 'having a greater position and larger stake in our city, not only than I deserve but probably than any citizen in our time, I feel more bound than any other man to give up all to my country, even my life.'

Before sailing from Vada in the Maremma on 11 December he received a despatch from the Signoria conferring on him plenary powers to negotiate with the King. Two Neapolitan galleys had been sent for him and he was received as an important guest rather than a suppliant when he landed a week later. Lorenzo was aware of the risk he was running, for a safe-conduct had not prevented King Ferrante from ordering the murder of Jacopo Piccinino, the condottiere; like Louis XI of France, Ferrante gloated over his prisoners and fed them like wild beasts. Nevertheless he was susceptible to logic, and Lorenzo was a master of cogent argument. There were several valid reasons for a treaty with Florence. Both the Pope and the King of France had claims on Naples which the Pope's nephews and the Angevins might revive. Since making peace with the Turks Venice might encourage their incursions into Neapolitan territory, whereas Florence could be a convenient ally and a financial bulwark.

There was a thriving Florentine colony at Naples, including artists and scholars as well as merchants and bankers, who had scarcely been affected by the recent hostilities. Though her husband had been fighting against Lorenzo and was still entrenched at Siena, the Duchess of Calabria and her brother-in-law Federigo admired him as a fine conversationalist and a sympathetic personality. This helped to sway the King, who gradually yielded to Lorenzo's charm though at first unconvinced by his arguments. Unwilling to offend the Pope and suspecting that Lorenzo's absence after his military setbacks might undermine his popularity at home, Ferrante procrastinated. His son Alfonso and the Pope were stubbornly opposed to a treaty: the former was determined to dominate Tuscany; the latter insisted that Lorenzo come to Rome and sue for pardon before any agreement was signed.

Lorenzo had no desire to venture from one lion's den to another, and even the King advised him not to go. But for all his sociability and the lavish entertainment of his Neapolitan hosts, he was deeply dejected during the three months he was forced to linger at Naples. Even when Ferrante agreed to sign a treaty he found further pretexts for delaying Lorenzo's departure, and Lorenzo felt he was in a gilded cage.

All the news he received from Florence was discouraging. His Venetian allies resented a separate treaty and had detached his ablest general, Roberto Malatesta, from his service. His protégés in the Romagna dreaded the loss of his patronage. The Florentines expected to be treated with all the honours – of a war they had lost. As Bartolommeo Scala, secretary of the Florentine Republic, wrote to him on 1 January 1480: 'Only to you would such extensive powers be given in so important a matter . . . Peace would be most welcome here, but if the conditions are not honourable you know our nature: we praise or blame according to which way the wind blows or our feelings move us. We do not trouble to reason.'

In spite of the armistice Lorenzo suspected that Alfonso of Calabria had instigated the Genoese Fregosi to grab Sarzana, which his father had acquired for its strategic value. This looked as if King Ferrante were playing a double game. Lorenzo could only brazen it out with his wit till a treaty was ratified in February.

Considering all the money Ferrante had squandered on the war, and the fact that his son had been victorious and Lorenzo was in his clutches, this was a diplomatic triumph for Lorenzo. At last he was free to sail from Naples, and though Ferrante tried to lure him back en route he reached home by the middle of March. Peace was jubilantly proclaimed in Florence on the Feast of the Annunciation with bonfires and the pealing of bells, and the miraculous image of the Madonna was carried in a procession from Impruneta. But the jubilation was ephemeral, for the terms of the treaty published on 17 March disappointed the Florentines, who could not realize the weakness of their position. Alfonso of Calabria still occupied Siena; and he hoped to keep the towns and fortresses he had captured in Tuscany. He was to receive an annual indemnity; the Pazzi prisoners at Volterra were to be released, and, most humiliating, Florence was to beg the Pope's pardon for its past offences. Sarzana was not even mentioned. As a neighbour in Siena, Alfonso of Calabria would be a permanent threat to Florence. Since taxes were increased to pay his indemnity, many citizens shared the opinion of Landucci, who wrote in his diary: 'We Florentines have the wise custom of giving money in payment to everyone who does us an injury, and who destroys and pillages our territory. And this is not a solitary instance; it will always be the same; anyone who wants money from the Florentines has only to do them an injury.'

As a result of the alliance between Florence and Naples, Venice made a separate treaty with the Pope. Though Sixtus was unable to struggle on without Neapolitan aid he refused to withdraw his interdict. And he insisted that Lorenzo should come to Rome.

Lorenzo and Florence were rescued from an unexpected quarter. Those legendary bogies, the Turks, who had been used so long as political scarecrows, materialized swiftly and suddenly in the kingdom of Naples. Some seven thousand landed at Otranto at the end of July and massacred the population. Of the 22,000 inhabitants 12,000 were slaughtered, the rest were enslaved. The old Archbishop, dragged from the altar where he had bravely implored Divine aid, was sawn in half beside the local commandant who shared his fate. A horde of prisoners who refused to embrace Islam were driven like sheep up a neighbouring hill to be slain and their corpses left for carrion. The news spread purple panic in Rome, where the Pope promised to pardon all the sins of Christians who fought the Turks under the banner of the Cross: he even considered escaping to Avignon. Alfonso of Calabria was recalled from Siena in a frenzy of frustration to extirpate the invaders, which he eventually succeeded in doing on 10 September 1481 – more than a year later. To a greater extent than was realized, his victory was due to Florentine loans and contributions.

So intimate had become the ties between Florence and Naples that King Ferrante's letters to Lorenzo overflowed with cordiality. Eschewing the usual formalities, he addressed him as 'Lorenzo my beloved friend'. And Lorenzo's letters to Giovanni Albino, the Neapolitan scholar employed as secretary and librarian by Alfonso of Calabria, were syrupy in their solicitude for the Duke's welfare, as when he wrote on 18 May 1481: 'Albino my dear and good brother, I cannot decide whether your letters of 2nd and 8th May give me more pleasure than pain. With the strongest desire for the fame of our Lord Duke, so well initiated with the drubbing of those Turkish dogs on the 18th, comes a fear lest His Lordship might suffer some accident by his valour. Those skirmishes you describe, in which His Lordship often takes part, made me turn pale more than once, for I have read and reread your letter. If possible, my Albino, send us news often, and beseech his Lordship to be cautious. I will say no more because I feel nervous as I write. Bid him take care of his person for the sake of God and himself, and for us his servants, and do what is needful at the risk of others rather than his own. You who are beside him must see to this even at the cost of your life, and if not on your account do it for mine, if you love me. Commend me to his Lordship. I anxiously await your reply to know whether my friendly exhortation has any effect without hindering what I regard as certain, which is that his Lordship will return from the expedition wreathed with laurels. So I expect from day to day to have your news.'

Since Alfonso had recently been master of Siena after besieging Colle and ravaging the Tuscan countryside, Lorenzo had turned the other cheek with a vengeance. Yet since Naples had become his ally he played his new role with unction. Ippolita Sforza, Alfonso's wife, had been his warmest advocate during his dangerous Neapolitan excursion – the King had called her Lorenzo's 'confederate' – and her letters prove her genuine affection for him. This might have contributed to his reconciliation with the crafty king. One is constantly amazed by the mutability of such relationships. As with the late Duke of Milan, Lorenzo had to make the best of a tortuous partner. While begging Alfonso to be cautious in fighting the Turks, he must have been grateful to the latter for ridding him of a piratical neighbour. Landucci, a typical Florentine, regarded the Turkish invasion as 'a great miracle'.

The most mortifying clause of the peace treaty was clinched at the end of 1480. Twelve eminent Florentines repaired to Rome to ask the Pope's forgiveness for whatever errors the Republic had committed, of which His Holiness was more cognizant than they. This was by no means the abject apology Sixtus desired, for the detested Lorenzo was not among the ambassadors, and there was to be no individual exclusion from his pardon and no question of indemnity. But Sixtus had no choice while the Turks were slaughtering Christians in Apulia: the infidels were far too close to Rome.

Appearances were saved by ceremonious splendour. On 3 December, the first Sunday in Advent, the ambassadors, led by Francesco Soderini, Bishop of Volterra, were received by the Pope seated on a throne surrounded by Cardinals outside the bronze gates of St Peter's. They knelt down to beg forgiveness and Luigi Guicciardini acted as their spokesman. So dense was the chattering throng that his words were inaudible. The Pope reprimanded the Florentines with a pompous display of righteous indignation and tapped each with a staff in token of chastisement and forgiveness to the chant of the *Miserere*. After his perfunctory blessing, the gates were opened and the penitents followed the Papal procession to attend High Mass.

Soon after Lorenzo's return from Naples a *Balìa* or *Consiglio Maggiore* (a large and representative Committee of Reform) was appointed to consider constitutional changes. The result was to tighten Medicean control by creating a new council of seventy members, the *Settanta*, nominally for five years but permanent in fact. The Seventy transacted business through two committees, one of eight members, the *Otto di Pratica*, for military and foreign affairs, and another of twelve members called *Procuratori*, to supervise financial and commercial affairs. The predominance of the Medici party was therefore assured, and during the rest of Lorenzo's life Florence was free from the immemorial curse of family feuds.

Even if we make allowances for his clerical bias, Ludwig Pastor's comment on Sixtus IV in his *History of the Popes* is comically ingenuous. 'It is profoundly regrettable,' he wrote, 'that the name of a Pope should be involved in this Conspiracy. Lorenzo had given Sixtus IV sufficient cause of discontent to justify declaring war against him. The principle of self-preservation required him to take strenuous measures, including the overthrow of a treacherous enemy, to guarantee the future, but it would have been worthier of a Pope to fight openly rather than to interfere in a coup d'état, even if this might be accomplished without bloodshed.'

Epilogue

ANOTHER plot to assassinate Lorenzo, probably instigated by Girolamo Riario, was hatched in Rome in May 1481; it was discovered and the conspirators were condemned to death. The Signoria passed a law making an attempt on Lorenzo's life high treason. A bodyguard was assigned to him. Henceforth his supremacy was officially recognized, though he bore no title save the honorific 'il Magnifico'. The government offices were filled with his adherents and the finances of the Medici became entangled with those of the Republic – a standing reproach from his opponents.

As long as Sixtus IV was alive there was little hope for peace in Italy. When the Peace of Bagnolo was signed in August 1484 after the war he had provoked between Venice and Ferrara, which he claimed as feudal suzerain – as usual for the sake of Girolamo Riario's aggrandizement – his fit of rage proved fatal.

The election of Cardinal Giovanni Battista Cibò, an easygoing Genoese patrician aged fifty-two, whose children he did not scruple to acknowledge, was providential for Florence. Innocent VIII was favourable to the Medici and attentive, if not subservient, to Lorenzo's advice. Lorenzo's eldest son Piero, now aged fourteen, was among the envoys sent to Rome to congratulate him. Warning Piero not to take precedence over any one older than himself in a letter of elaborate instructions, Lorenzo emphasized: 'though you are my son, you are a citizen of Florence (like your elders).' Piero was urged to commend his younger brother Giovanni to the notice of the new Pope, for already the child's future as a prince of the Church was close to Lorenzo's heart. Referring to the Pazzi Conspiracy, he wrote: 'Add that I have experienced how hurtful it has been to be out of favour with the late Pontiff although, as it seems to me, I was unjustly persecuted rather for the sins of others than for any insult or offence to him of holy memory. But I leave this to the judgment of posterity.'

Although he seemed full of nervous energy, Lorenzo had inherited his father's gout. Often he had to retire from public affairs to take cures which afforded him only temporary relief. Before he was forty he looked much older. Yet the recovery of Sarzana in 1487 was mainly due to his personal exertion. His presence encouraged the troops during the final attack, and he saw to it that the garrison and inhabitants were spared the usual pillage and destruction.

Soon after the recapture of Sarzana Lorenzo's second daughter, Maddalena, was betrothed to Franceschetto Cibò, the boorish son of Innocent VIII, and his own son Piero to Alfonsina, the daughter of Roberto Orsini, Count of Tagliacozzo and d'Alba, descended from a different branch of his mother Clarice's family but equally powerful. (Roberto, a Grand Constable of the kingdom of Naples, had previously died of the plague.) Maddalena's marriage in January 1488 smoothed the way towards Giovanni's clerical promotion, but her husband, accustomed to Roman pomp and luxury, complained that he felt mortified by the modest homeliness of his reception in Florence. A chronicler recorded that he was 'received with great splendour and lodged with all his people right royally. But soon Lorenzo, taking pleasure in seeing his son-in-law familiarly, or perchance thinking to gain still more the Pope's benevolence, constantly invited him to dine at his house without ceremony, or as we say *alla casalinga*. Now it appears that the Florentines are generally held to be chary of spending their money, so he thought that those gentlemen who had accompanied him to honour his wedding might be treated in like manner, and was sore troubled, fearing that the city of Florence and his relations would be held up to ridicule afterwards in Rome.'* The homely Tuscan cooking did not appeal to Franceschetto's palate. Food and money were his chief preoccupations.

In April 1488 – a decade after the Pazzi Conspiracy – its leading sponsor, Girolamo Riario, was assassinated by two of his courtiers, Lorenzo and Cecco Orsi (or d'Orso), who stabbed him as he was leaning against an open window of his palace at Forlì. His corpse, like that of the Florentine conspirators, was flung into the square below and dragged through the streets by his long-suffering subjects. Giuliano had been avenged, but there is no proof that Lorenzo had instigated the murder, as Count Pasolini maintained in his biography of Caterina Sforza, Riario's ruthless widow. On the contrary, he treated Caterina with a chivalry she scarcely deserved, and the assassins were thoroughly snubbed when they tried to curry favour with him. Caterina caused the old father of the Orsi to be executed with every refinement of cruelty. After the murder of her second husband, a monster called Giacomo Feo, she married a Medici of the cadet branch and cousin of Lorenzo, Giovanni, to whom she bore the famous condottiere Giovanni delle Bande Nere, father of Cosimo the first Grand Duke of Tuscany.

Clarice died on 30 July in the same year after nineteen years of marriage. She had long been suffering from consumption but her death came suddenly while Lorenzo was absent at the baths of Filetta. Though he had appreciated her domestic virtues his passions were reserved for other ladies married or single. His liaison with Bartolommea de' Nasi, a matron more gentle than comely, was notorious. He would often gallop from the country to spend a night with her in town, returning before daylight. The death of his mother

* *Vita e Fatti d'Innocenzio VIII*, Scritta per Messer Francesco Serdonati, fiorentino, etc. Milano, Ferrario, 1829, 59 *et seq.* (Quoted from Janet Ross: *Lives of the Early Medici*, London 1910.)

Lucrezia in 1482 had been a heavier blow. 'Besides losing a mother, at the mere thought of whom my heart breaks,' he wrote, 'I have lost the counsellor who relieved me of many a burden.' And his third daughter, Luigia, had died not long before Clarice.

Lorenzo's grief was mitigated by the news that his second son, Giovanni, would soon be promoted to the Cardinalate. At the age of fourteen he was already provided with rich benefices, abbacies, bishoprics and archbishoprics. His nomination in March 1489 was to have been kept secret for three years, and the Pope was annoyed by the publicity it received in Florence. In a letter of thanks to Innocent, Lorenzo explained: 'As to keeping this affair secret I should be much distressed if the knowledge of it had been made public by me. But Your Holiness may rest assured that it was immediately known in Rome, and then divulged by letters to people here, so that every one came to congratulate me. I can confirm that the news was not published by me, nor did I cause any demonstration of joy to be made. In any case, whether by my fault or not, I am extremely distressed that Your Holiness should have experienced any annoyance, and can only promise in the future to carry out to the letter any commands Your Holiness deigns to give me.'

Lorenzo's health, like that of Pope Innocent, was deteriorating rapidly, and he could hardly wait for the three years to pass until Giovanni's initiation. By then he was far too ill to attend the ceremonies in the abbey church of Fiesole and later in the Cathedral. He was carried into the banqueting hall of the palace to greet his guests, with a premonition that he would never see his favourite son again. Realizing that death was near, he sent Giovanni a long paternal letter full of political wisdom, worldly knowledge, and fatherly foresight. 'As you are now going to Rome, the very sink of iniquity,' he wrote, 'the difficulty of following my advice will naturally be greater; for not only does example have its influence, but you will have no lack of evil counsellors and tempters.'

Lorenzo's efforts to keep the peace between the vacillating Pope Innocent and the perfidious King of Naples were crowned with success in February 1492. As the ally of both, he had been driven to such a pitch of exasperation that he said he longed to retire for six months to some quiet hermitage where no breath of Italian politics could reach his ears.

Some of his last letters to Rome were written in defence of his young friend, Pico della Mirandola, the mystical philosopher who had been accused of heresy by a Papal commission. To his ambassador, Giovanni Lanfredini, he wrote on 19 June 1489: 'The Count della Mirandola is here leading a most saintly life, like a monk. He has been and is now occupied in writing admirable theological works: commentaries and psalms and other excellent books on theology. He recites the ordinary priest's office, observes all fasts and absolute chastity; has but a small retinue and lives quite simply with only what is necessary. To me he appears an example to other men. He is anxious to be absolved from what little contumacy is still attributed to him by the Holy Father and to have a Brief by which His Holiness accepts him as a son and a good Christian, he persevering in a Christian life. I greatly desire that this satisfaction be given to him, for there are few men I love better or esteem more. I feel certain that he is a devout and faithful Christian, and his conduct is such that the whole city would vouch for him. Do all you can to obtain this Brief in such a form that it may comfort his conscience. This would be not less agreeable to me than any one of the many services you have rendered, and for which I am most grateful.'

Ironically it was Pope Innocent's Borgia successor, Alexander VI, who sent the Brief of absolution. St Thomas More's translation of Pico's biography introduced him to English readers, of whom Walter Pater was most percipient when he wrote: 'The Renaissance of the fifteenth century was, in many things, greater by what it designed than by what it achieved.'

On the subject of Florence during Lorenzo's latter years Guicciardini concluded: 'The city enjoyed perfect peace. The citizens in whose hands rested the administration of affairs held firmly together; the government, carried on and supported by them, was so powerful that no one dared openly to oppose it. The people were daily entertained with festivals and novelties; trade and business were at the height of prosperity. Men of talent found their proper place in the great liberality with which the arts and sciences were promoted, and those who practised them were honoured. This city, quiet and peaceful at home, enjoyed also great consideration abroad, because she had a government whose head had full authority; because she had lately extended her dominions, and been mainly instrumental in preserving Ferrara and King Ferrante, because she had complete control over the Pope, and because, in conjunction with Naples and Milan, she in a measure kept all Italy in equilibrium.'

For 'talent' we may substitute 'genius' in the superlative examples of Leonardo da Vinci and Michelangelo Buonarroti. At the age of fifteen Michelangelo was taken by Lorenzo into the Medici palace, where a room was assigned to him and he was supplied with clothes and pocket money. At meals Lorenzo sat at the head of the table and whoever came first sat next to him, regardless of rank. Thus the adolescent Michelangelo often had the place of honour, and met some of the finest contemporary poets, philosophers, and scholars in Italy. Lorenzo showed him his rare cameos and medals, and he chiselled and moulded in the garden of San Marco, then an open-air studio full of sculpture directed by Bertoldo, Donatello's pupil. Poliziano introduced him to classical antiquity and inspired him to produce his marble relief known as the *Battle of the Centaurs*, representing the rape of Hippodamia by the centaur Eurytus, a gloriously rhythmic tangle of naked bodies and a precursor, as Dr Charles de Tolnay pointed out, of 'the great multiple-figure compositions, such as the *Battle of Cascina* and the *Last Judgment.*'

There was but one discord, rising shriller, amid this apparent harmony. Hitherto the Convent of San Marco had been a spiritual annexe of the Medici palace: Cosimo had engaged Michelozzo to rebuild it and he had founded its splendid library. Often he retired to a cell there for prayer and meditation, despite his saying that 'a government cannot be maintained by paternosters.' The Dominicans had always been friends of the family. But recently a Ferrarese friar had come to San Marco without any enthusiasm for the arts or the revival of learning, though he had been recommended to Lorenzo by Pico della Mirandola.

Fra Girolamo Savonarola could only see corruption on every side of him, for which he held Lorenzo responsible. His sensational denunciations of sin and calls to repentance were loud with political implications and he claimed the divine gift of prophecy. In July 1491 he was elected Prior of San Marco. It had been customary for the new prior to pay a formal visit to the head of the house to which it was so largely indebted, but Savonarola refused to do so on the ground that he owed his election to God alone. 'You see, a stranger has come into my house, and he does not think me fit to visit,' said Lorenzo, whose conciliatory gestures were invariably repulsed by the arrogant friar.

Savonarola continued to denounce the vices of the age in violent language, and to threaten dire retribution. When five prominent citizens advised him to moderate his speech 'for the sake of the common good and peace of the city', he answered: 'I see that you are sent to me by Lorenzo. Tell him to repent of his sins, for the Lord spares no one and fears not the princes of the earth. . . . Though I am a stranger and Lorenzo the first citizen, it is he who is to depart, and I who am to remain.' And he predicted the speedy deaths of Lorenzo, the Pope, and the King of Naples.

Lorenzo's attacks of gout became more agonizing and frequent. The various cures he had tried were ineffective, which is hardly surprising when we read the advice of such doctors as the following:

'My medicine is a conserve made up in solid form called *ellescof*, half an ounce is to be taken at sunrise once a month, particularly when Your Magnificence feels any pain. In order to prevent the return of these pains you must get a stone called sapphire, and have it set in gold, so that it should touch the skin. This must be worn on the third finger of the left hand. If this is done the pains in the joints, or gouty pains, will cease, because that stone has occult virtues, and the specific one of preventing evil humours going to the joints. . . . Afterwards in the summer, in the month of August, I will find celandine, which is a red stone that grows in the stomach of the swallow. I will send it to Your Magnificence to be tied in a piece of linen and sewn in your shirt under the left breast at the nipple. This will have the same effect as the sapphire aforementioned, and thus *Deo Duce* Your Magnificence will be freed of and secure from every pain in the joints . . .'

Ellescof, sapphire, celandine, and the waters of Morba brought him no relief: the disease spread all over his body and was aggravated by a burning fever. At the beginning of 1492 he was too ill to attend to business. But he could not complain, like his grandfather Cosimo, that his palace was too large for so small a family. Besides his sisters Bianca and Nannina, he had three sons and three daughters: Piero, his eldest son who succeeded him; Giovanni who became Pope Leo X; Giuliano, who became Duke of Nemours; Maddalena, who married Franceschetto Cibò; Lucrezia, who married Giacomo Salviati; and Contessina, who married Pietro Ridolfi.

On 21 March he was taken to his quiet villa at Careggi, attended by his favourite daughter Lucrezia, his son Piero, and the devoted Poliziano who left the most reliable account of his last hours. When forced to realize that his plight was hopeless, he insisted on rising from his bed, in spite of protests, to receive the last sacrament. Having been dressed by his weeping attendants he fell on his knees and cried: 'I will not suffer that my Lord and God should thus come to me.' After he had received absolution, all who had been present withdrew except his son Piero, to whom, according to Poliziano, he said: 'The citizens will doubtless recognize you as my successor, nor do I doubt that you will obtain the same authority as I myself have exercised. But since the collective State is a body with many heads, remember always to follow that course which appears to be the most honourable, and study rather the general welfare than individual and private interests.' He then gave instructions about the funeral, that he should be buried without pomp in a manner suitable to a private citizen.

In addition to his private physician Piero Leoni, Lodovico il Moro had sent him Lazaro of Pavia, who had a great reputation in Milan. Lazaro prescribed a concoction of pulverized pearls and precious stones which probably hastened his end. While he swallowed this potion he gazed tenderly at Poliziano, who turned away to hide his tears. Lorenzo then asked for Pico della Mirandola. Why had he not come to see him? So Pico was summoned and Lorenzo apologized for the trouble he was causing: he would die more happily now that he had seen him. From the description of Pico translated by St Thomas More and quoted by Walter Pater, we may imagine that his presence might comfort a dying man, for he was 'of feature and shape seemly and beauteous, of stature goodly and high, of flesh tender and soft, his visage lovely and fair, his colour white, intermingled with comely reds, his eyes grey, and quick of look, his teeth white and even, his hair yellow and abundant.' Contrasting with the gloom of Lorenzo's woebegone familiars so angelic an apparition brought cheerful intimations of immortality. With Pico and Poliziano he rallied awhile, regretting that he should not live to complete their libraries and see the manuscripts which Lascaris was bringing from Greece.

It was probably Pico who sent his friend Savonarola to Lorenzo's deathbed – a visit which gave rise to conflicting accounts, some tinted with propaganda. After exhorting Lorenzo to cling to the Faith, to amend his life, and to meet death with fortitude, Savonarola was about to retire when Lorenzo asked for his blessing and joined in his prayers, serene amid the sorrow of those around him. He died on 8 April 1492, in his forty-fourth year.

All kinds of sinister portent accompanied his death, exaggerated by superstitious rumour. His doctor Piero Leoni was subsequently drowned in a well: the facts pointed to suicide, but rumour again attributed his death to the vengeance of Lorenzo's heirs. Leoni's treatment had not been approved by his Milanese colleague, who objected that the patient needed refrigeratives whereas the remedies prescribed had been calorific. There seems to have been little to choose between them. Since Leoni had never believed the disease mortal the shock might have unhinged him.

Lorenzo's body was moved from Careggi to the Convent of San Marco – apparently Savonarola raised no objection – until he was interred in the old sacristy of San Lorenzo. In 1559 his remains were moved to the new sacristy and buried under Michelangelo's statue of the Madonna beside his murdered brother Giuliano.

Lorenzo had been a paragon of pacifism in a period of extensive petty warfare – less petty for the peasantry whose fields were ravaged than for the citizens burdened with taxes to pay for the bands of mercenaries. The Pazzi Conspiracy had lured him into a campaign which caught the Florentines unprepared, yet he had overcome a disastrous defeat by sheer personal magnetism after sailing into a potential death-trap, an act of courage which his detractors could not deny. As the leading statesman who struggled to keep the peace of Italy his merit was outstanding. But his cultural significance transcended his age. More than any contemporary he was a cosmopolitan Italian with a sense of the fundamental meaning of existence, enriching the minds of others as well as his own. He was the most versatile representative of an entire epoch. And in his restless search for an elusive ideal his spirit was curiously modern.

List of Illustrations

List of Illustrations

Index

Numerals in italics refer to illustrations

126

Index